# Renewable Energy Technologies

AUTHORS

**Prof. Sanjay Agrawal**
*Vice Chancellor and Professor*
Department of Electrical Engineering,
Swami Vivekanand Technical University,
Bhilai, Chhattisgarh

**Dr. Rajeev Kumar Mishra**
*Associate Professor,*
Department of Applied Sciences (Physics),
Galgotias College of Engineering and
Technology, Greater Noida, Uttar Pradesh

REVIEWER

**Dr. Suram Singh Verma**
*Professor,*
Sant Longowal Institute of Engineering and Technology,
SLIET, Longowal, Distt.-Sangrur, Punjab

KHANNA BOOK
PUBLISHING CO. (P) Ltd.
4C/4344, Ansari Road, Darya Ganj,
New Delhi, India

All India Council for
Technical Education
Nelson Mandela Marg, Vasant Kunj,
New Delhi, India

Dear Readers,

To prevent the piracy, this book is secured with HIGH SECURITY HOLOGRAM on the front title cover. In case you don't find the hologram on the front cover title, please write us to at contact@khannabooks.com or whatsapp us at +91-99109 09320 and avail special gift voucher for yourself.

Specimen of Hologram on front Cover title:

Moreover, there is a SPECIAL DISCOUNT COUPON for you with EVERY HOLOGRAM.
How to avail this SPECIAL DISCOUNT:
Step 1: Scratch the hologram
Step 2: Under the scratch area, your "coupon code" is available
Step 3: Logon to www.khannabooks.com
Step 4: Use your "coupon code" in the shopping cart and get your copy at a special discount
Step 5: Enjoy your reading!

**ISBN:** 978-93-5538-718-9
**Book Code:** DIP446EN

**Renewable Energy Technologies**
*by* Prof. Sanjay Agrawal and
Dr. Rajeev Kumar Mishra

**First Edition:** 2025

*Originally Published by:*
**All India Council for Technical Education, Ministry of Education, GOI**

*Exclusively Published & Distributed by:*
**Khanna Book Publishing Co. (P) Ltd.**
4C/4344, Ansari Road, Daryaganj,
New Delhi (INDIA)

Visit us at: **www.khannabooks.com**
Write us at: **contact@khannabooks.com**

To view complete list of books,
Please scan the QR Code:
KPH

*Printed in Bharat.*

प्रो. टी. जी. सीताराम
अध्यक्ष
Prof. T. G. Sitharam
Chairman

सत्यमेव जयते

आज़ादी का अमृत महोत्सव

अखिल भारतीय तकनीकी शिक्षा परिषद्
(भारत सरकार का एक सांविधिक निकाय)
(शिक्षा मंत्रालय, भारत सरकार)
नेल्सन मंडेला मार्ग, वसंत कुंज, नई दिल्ली–110070
दूरभाष : 011–26131498
ई–मेल : chairman@aicte-india.org

ALL INDIA COUNCIL FOR TECHNICAL EDUCATION
(A STATUTORY BODY OF THE GOVT. OF INDIA)
(Ministry of Education, Govt. of India)
Nelson Mandela Marg, Vasant Kunj, New Delhi-110070
Phone : 011-26131498
E-mail : chairman@aicte-india.org

# FOREWORD

Engineers are the backbone of any modern society. They are the ones responsible for the marvels as well as the improved quality of life across the world. Engineers have driven humanity towards greater heights in a more evolved and unprecedented manner.

The All India Council for Technical Education (AICTE), have spared no efforts towards the strengthening of the technical education in the country. AICTE is always committed towards promoting quality Technical Education to make India a modern developed nation emphasizing on the overall welfare of mankind.

An array of initiatives has been taken by AICTE in last decade which have been accelerated now by the National Education Policy (NEP) 2020. The implementation of NEP under the visionary leadership of Hon'ble Prime Minister of India envisages the provision for education in regional languages to all, thereby ensuring that every graduate becomes competent enough and is in a position to contribute towards the national growth and development through innovation & entrepreneurship.

One of the spheres where AICTE had been relentlessly working since past couple of years is providing high quality original technical contents at Under Graduate & Diploma level prepared and translated by eminent educators in various Indian languages to its aspirants. For students pursuing 2$^{nd}$ year of their Engineering education, AICTE has identified 87 books, which shall be translated into 12 Indian languages - Hindi, Tamil, Gujarati, Odia, Bengali, Kannada, Urdu, Punjabi, Telugu, Marathi, Assamese & Malayalam. In addition to the English medium, books in different Indian Languages are going to support the students to understand the concepts in their respective mother tongue.

On behalf of AICTE, I express sincere gratitude to all distinguished authors, reviewers and translators from the renowned institutions of high repute for their admirable contribution in a record span of time.

AICTE is confident that these outcomes based original contents shall help aspirants to master the subject with comprehension and greater ease.

(Prof. T. G. Sitharam)

## ACKNOWLEDGEMENT

The authors are grateful to the authorities of AICTE, particularly Prof. T. G. Sitharam, Chairman; Dr. Abhay Jere, Vice-Chairman; Prof. Rajive Kumar, Member-Secretary and Dr Amit Kumar Srivastava, Director, Faculty Development Cell for their planning to publish the book entitled "*Renewable Energy Technologies*." We sincerely acknowledge the valuable contributions of the reviewer of the book Dr. S. S. Verma, Professor, Department of Physics, SLIET, Longowal, Punjab for providing invaluable inputs in all units of the book.

We would also like to extend our thank to Prof. Nageshwar Rao, Vice-Chancellor, IGNOU, New Delhi, Prof. M. K. Verma, Vice-Chancellor, Chhattisgarh Swami Vivekanand Technical University, Bhilai, Chhattisgarh; Prof. Pradeep Kumar Mishra, Vice-Chancellor, AKTU, Lucknow, Prof. Rajesh Tripathi, HOD, Applied Sciences, GCET, Gr. Noida for their constant support and encouragement during the preparation of the book.

Sincere thanks to our colleagues, friends and family members for their co-operation and moral support at every stage of this book.

We are tankful to the AICTE members, experts and authors whoshared their opinion and thought to make this book better. Acknowledgements are also to the contributors and experts in the field of renewable energy whose published books, review articles, papers, photographs, footnotes, references, and other valuable information enriched us at the time of writing the book.

Any suggestions for further improvement of the book will be acknowledged and well appreciated.

**Prof. Sanjay Agrawal**

**Dr. Rajeev Kumar Mishra**

# PREFACE

We feel an immense pleasure to present the book entitled "*Renewable Energy Technologies*". This book is an outcome the extensive experience of the authors and the reviewer in the area of renewable energy. The book is written as per the syllabus of Diploma, 2nd year provided by AICTE.

In the view of the explosive technological development in the field of renewable energy in last few decades, the fundamental knowledge of renewable energy is necessary for the students. The main objective of writing this book is to discussthe basics of renewable energy technologies to the diploma students, enable them to get an insight of the subject. Efforts have been done to explain the fundamental concepts of the subject in a simple manner.

In the process of writing various units of the book, we have taken the references of standard text books, recent published papers, the latest information available on relevant websites.Together with the fundamental knowledge, the book coversadvance development in the subject area.It is important to note that in all the units we have provided a QR Code to collect additional knowledge on the specific topic.

This book "*Renewable Energy Technologies*" is meant to provide a thorough knowledgeof renewableenergy on the topics covered. This book will also prepare the students to apply the knowledge to meet the challenges of protecting the environment and providing solutions for the development of clean and green energy.

**Prof. Sanjay Agrawal**

**Dr. Rajeev Kumar Mishra**

# OUTCOME BASED EDUCATION

For the implementation of an outcome based education the first requirement is to develop an outcome based curriculum and incorporate an outcome based assessment in the education system. By going through outcome based assessments, evaluators will be able to evaluate whether the students have achieved the outlined standard, specific and measurable outcomes. With the proper incorporation of outcome based education there will be a definite commitment to achieve a minimum standard for all learners without giving up at any level. At the end of the programme running with the aid of outcome based education, a student will be able to arrive at the following outcomes:

Programme Outcomes (POs) are statements that describe what students are expected to know and be able to do upon graduating from the program. These relate to the skills, knowledge, analytical ability, attitude and behaviour that students acquire through the program. The POs essentially indicate what the students can do from subject-wise knowledge acquired by them during the program. As such, POs define the professional profile of an engineering diploma graduate.

National Board of Accreditation (NBA) has defined the following seven POs for an Engineering diploma graduate:

**PO-1. Basic and Discipline specific knowledge:** Apply knowledge of basic mathematics, science and engineering fundamentals and engineering specialization to solve the engineering problems.

**PO-2. Problem analysis:** Identify and analyses well-defined engineering problems using codified standard methods.

**PO-3. Design/development of solutions:** Design solutions for well-defined technical problems and assist with the design of systems components or processes to meet specified needs.

**PO-4. Engineering Tools, Experimentation and Testing:** Apply modern engineering tools and appropriate technique to conduct standard tests and measurements.

**PO-5. Engineering practices for society, sustainability and environment:** Apply appropriate technology in context of society, sustainability, environment and ethical practices.

**PO-6. Project Management:** Use engineering management principles individually, as a team member or a leader to manage projects and effectively communicate about well-defined engineering activities.

**PO-7. Life-long learning:** Ability to analyse individual needs and engage in updating in the context of technological changes.

# COURSE OUTCOMES

After completion of the course the students will be able to:

**CO-1:** Maintain the optimised working of solar PV and CS power plants.

**CO-2:** Maintain the optimised working of large wind power plants.

**CO-3:** Maintain the optimised working of small wind turbines.

**CO-4:** Maintain the optimised working of micro hydro power plants.

**CO-5:** Maintain the optimised working of biomass-based power plants.

Mapping of Course Outcomes with Programme Outcomes to be done according to the matrix given below:

| Course Outcomes | EXPECTED MAPPING WITH PROGRAMME OUTCOMES (1- Weak Correlation; 2- Medium Correlation; 3- Strong Correlation) | | | | | | |
|---|---|---|---|---|---|---|---|
| | PO-1 | PO-2 | PO-3 | PO-4 | PO-5 | PO-6 | PO-7 |
| CO-1 | 3 | 3 | 2 | 2 | 1 | 2 | 3 |
| CO-2 | 3 | 2 | 2 | 1 | - | 1 | 3 |
| CO-3 | 3 | 3 | 2 | 1 | - | 1 | 3 |
| CO-4 | 3 | 3 | 3 | 2 | 1 | 2 | 3 |
| CO-5 | 3 | 3 | 2 | 1 | 1 | 2 | 3 |

## GUIDELINES FOR TEACHERS

To implement Outcome Based Education (OBE) knowledge level and skill set of the students should be enhanced. Teachers should take a major responsibility for the proper implementation of OBE. Some of the responsibilities (not limited to) for the teachers in OBE system may be as follows:

- Within reasonable constraint, they should manoeuvre time to the best advantage of all students.
- They should assess the students only upon certain defined criterion without considering any other potential ineligibility to discriminate them.
- They should try to grow the learning abilities of the students to a certain level before they leave the institute.
- They should try to ensure that all the students are equipped with the quality knowledge as well as competence after they finish their education.
- They should always encourage the students to develop their ultimate performance capabilities.
- They should facilitate and encourage group work and team work to consolidate newer approach.
- They should follow Blooms taxonomy in every part of the assessment.

### Bloom's Taxonomy

| Level | Teacher should Check | Student should be able to | Possible Mode of Assessment |
|---|---|---|---|
| Creating | Students ability to create | Design or Create | Mini project |
| Evaluating | Students ability to Justify | Argue or Defend | Assignment |
| Analysing | Students ability to distinguish | Differentiate or Distinguish | Project/Lab Methodology |
| Applying | Students ability to use information | Operate or Demonstrate | Technical Presentation/ Demonstration |
| Understanding | Students ability to explain the ideas | Explain or Classify | Presentation/Seminar |
| Remembering | Students ability to recall (or remember) | Define or Recall | Quiz |

## GUIDELINES FOR STUDENTS

Students should take equal responsibility for implementing the OBE. Some of the responsibilities (not limited to) for the students in OBE system are as follows:

- Students should be well aware of each UO before the start of a unit in each and every course.
- Students should be well aware of each CO before the start of the course.
- Students should be well aware of each PO before the start of the programme.
- Students should think critically and reasonably with proper reflection and action.
- Learning of the students should be connected and integrated with practical and real life consequences.
- Students should be well aware of their competency at every level of OBE.

# LIST OF FIGURES

## LIST OF TABLES

# CONTENTS

# 1 Introduction

## UNIT SPECIFICS

In this unit following major points have been discussed:

- Present status of energy production in the world and in India
- Utilization of different energy generated by various sources
- Scenario of Conventional energy resources reserves in the World and in India
- Renewable Energy Potential of the World and India
- Effects of Renewable Energy use on the Environment
- Economical Aspects of Renewable Energy Utilization

The discussion in this chapter isbased on the current data available through various recognized agencies. Data based analysis is always easy and better to compare different technologies.

Besides, a large number of multiplechoice questions as well as questions of short and long answer types marked in two categories following lower and higher order of Bloom's taxonomy are given. A list of references and suggested readings are given in the unit so that the reader can go through them for practice. It is important to note that for getting more information on various topics of interest some QR codes have been provided in different sections which can be scanned for relevant supportive knowledge.

There is a "Know More" sectionat the end of the unit. This section has been carefully designed so that the supplementary information provided in this part becomes beneficial for the users of the book.

## RATIONALE

Energy is one of the basic needs of human being. It may be considered as the key parameter for the economic and industrial growth of a country. Energy, environment and economic development are closely related. The environmental problems like air pollution, water pollution, climate change, global warming etc are also closely linked with the energy production and its consumption.

In this chapter we shall talk about the different forms of energy, their production and use. The energy scenario of world and India will also be discussed. The economic aspects of renewable energy use will also be discussed with the help of suitable example.

## PRE-REQUISITES

Understanding of the unit conversion of energy

## UNIT OUTCOMES

List of outcomes of this unit is as follows:

U1-O1: To know about different types of energy resources.

U1-O2: To Know about reserves of primary energy resources.

U1-O3: To learn about the India's and World's renewable energy scenario.

U1-O4: To understand the effect of renewable energy on environment.

U1-O5: To analyse the economics of renewable energy use.

| Unit-1 Outcomes | EXPECTED MAPPING WITH COURSE OUTCOMES (1-Weak Correlation; 2-Medium Correlation; 3-Strong Correlation) | | | | |
|---|---|---|---|---|---|
| | CO-1 | CO-2 | CO-3 | CO-4 | CO-5 |
| U1-O1 | 3 | 3 | 3 | 3 | 3 |
| U1-O2 | 3 | 3 | 3 | 3 | 3 |
| U1-O3 | 3 | 3 | 3 | 3 | 3 |
| U1-O4 | 3 | 3 | 3 | 3 | 3 |
| U1-O5 | 3 | 3 | 3 | 3 | 3 |

## 1.1 OVERVIEW

Energy measures the ability to do work. It is measured/expressed in Joule (J), Watt-hour (Wh), Kilowatt-hour (kWh), Tetra Watt-hour (TWh) etc. Energyis essentially required for most of the activities of the modern society. Energy is an important parameter for the industrial, economic and social development of any country. It's utilization may be considered as one of the deciding factors for degree of development of a country. The global energy demand is increasing day by day because of the increase in population, industrialization and living standard of human beings. Most of the energy requirements of the world are being fulfilled by burning fossil fuels like coal, oil and natural gas but these resources are limited in stock and also depleting at a very fast rate. Therefore, we need to think about other sources of energy which are available in unlimited stock all around the world. These energy resources are known as renewable energy resources.

## 1.2 CLASSIFICATION OF ENERGY RESOURCES

The sources from which energy can be extracted are calledenergy resources. Depending on its nature, availability and storing capacity energy resources can be classified as:

### 1.2.1 Commercial and Non-commercial Energy Resources

These are also known as primary energy resources. These are available in nature in raw form e.g. coal, natural gas, oil, petroleum, nuclear power, air and water. The resources which are freelyavailable in nature like solar, agriculture waste etc. are known as non-commercial energy resources.

### 1.2.2 Conventional or Non-renewable Energy Resources

These are the energy resources which have been used for a long time. These resources are limited instock and exhaustible. These resources are depleting with time and may be used completely with no amount left. These causes pollution as they emit chemicals and hazardous gases like CO, $CO_2$, $N_2O$, $CH_4$, acid rain etc. Examples: Coal, Petroleum and Natural Gas.

### 1.2.3 Non-conventional or Renewable Energy Resources

Non-conventional or renewable energy resources are still in development stage of use. These resources can be renewed and used again and again. These are unlimited in stock and are inexhaustible. These energy resources when used usually cause no pollution and are environmentally friendly and sustainable in nature. Examples: Solar, Wind, Hydropower, Biomass, Geothermal, Wave, Tidal etc.
The detailed classification of energy resources is presented in Table 1.1

**Table 1.1:** Classification of energy resources

| Commercial | Conventional/ Non-Renewable | Non-conventional/ Renewable |
|---|---|---|
| • Also known as primary energy resources.<br>• Are available in nature in raw form.<br>**Examples:** coal, natural gas, oil, petroleum, nuclear power, air and water. | • Have been used for a long time.<br>• Are limited in stock and exhaustible.<br>• Depleting with time and may be used completely with no amount left.<br>• Causes pollution as they emitchemicals and hazardous gases like CO, $CO_2$, $N_2O$, $CH_4$, acid rain.<br>**Examples:** Coal, Petroleum and Natural Gas. | • Are still in development stage of use.<br>• Can be renewed and used again and again.<br>• Are unlimited in stock and are inexhaustible.<br>• Usuallycauses no pollution when used.<br>• Areenvironmentally friendly and sustainable in nature.<br>**Examples:** Solar, Wind, Hydropower, biomass, geothermal, wave, tidal etc. |

## 1.3 RESERVES OF ENERGY RESOURCES

Reserves of energy resources are the deposits (not-yet-extracted) of natural resources like coal, oil and natural gas.

### 1.3.1 Coal Reserves

The dead plants, under the influence of heat and high pressure for long duration of time, changes into a carbon-rich black or brownish rock better known as coal. Coal is one of the largest and primary sources of commercial energy worldwide. Coal is majorly used in thermal power plants to generate electricity. In thermal power plants, coal is burnt to generate water steam in the boiler and then this steam is used to run the turbine which drives the generator.

Based on carbon content, calorific value (amount of heat energy contained) and hardness, coal can be classifiedin its different varieties as: Anthracite, Bituminous, Lignite and Peat.

- **Anthracite:** Anthracite comes in the highest rank of the coal. This has very less volatile matter and moisture content. The ash content is also very small in Anthracite. The calorific value is about 8500-8700 kcal/kg. This coal is hard, brittle and lustrous in appearance. The carbon content in this category of coal is about 90-98%. It is mainly used in furnaces and water filtration systems.

In India, Anthracite deposits are located in Kashmir and Eastern Himalayas region. Formation: 300-360 million years old.

- **Bituminous:** Bituminous coals are black or dark grey in colour. Their average calorific value is about 4200-8500 kcal/kg. The carbon content in this category of coal varies from 70-86%. It comes in the middle rank of the coal and mainly used in thermal power plants for electricity generation and in steel production.

  In India bituminous coal deposits are available in Bihar, Bengal, Odisha and Madhya Pradesh. Formation: 100-300 million years old.
- **Lignite:** Lignite variety comes in the lowest rank of the coal. Ligniteis also famous as brown coal because of its brown colour. It is soft and contains 35-55% of moisture. The calorific value is about 4000-4200 kcal/kg. It has very low heating value, and is mainly used in electricity generation. In India, Lignite sites are in Tamil Nadu, Kashmir and Rajasthan. Formation: ~250 million years old.
- **Peat:** Peat is formed in the first stage of the coalification of coal from wood. Moisture content is more than 75% and can be used as fuel after drying. The carbon content is less than 60% and is an uneconomical fuel to use. Its calorific value is about 3500 kcal/kg on dry basis. In India, peat reserves are in the region of Nilgiri hills.

  About 70% of the coal reserves are made up of anthracite and bituminous coal varieties which are mainly used in power generational and metallurgy.

#### 1.3.1.1 India's Coal Reserves

Coal is one of the very important fossil fuels in India. It fulfils about 55% of country's energy demand. India is the second highest coal producing country in the world and fifth world's largest country in terms of coal deposits. The 27 major coalfields producing hard coal are confined to eastern and south-central part of the country. About 90% of the Lignite reserves arepresentin the coalfields of Tamil Nadu.Further, Jharkhand, Odisha, Chhattisgarh, West Bengal and Madhya Pradesh are five states having major coal reserves in India.

The chart in Fig. 1.1 represents the percentage share of the major states to the India's total coal reserves. Jharkhand has the most coal reserves followed by Odisha and Chhattisgarh.

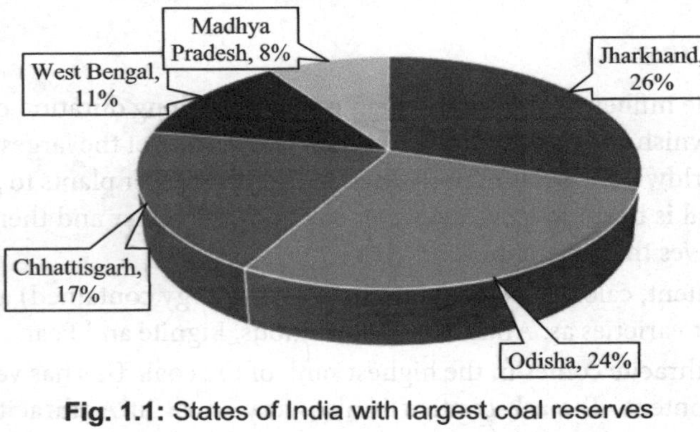


**Fig. 1.1:** States of India with largest coal reserves

### 1.3.1.2 World's Coal Reserves

World coal reserves are about 1 billion tonnes in 2020 with major shares of US, Russia, Australia, China and India. Despite concerns about air pollution and greenhouse gas emission, coal use is likely to continue to be significant in the near future. Country wise coal reserves in first ten leading countries aregiven in Table 1.2.At current consumption rate and excluding unproven reserves, world has about 140 years of coal left. The percentage share of the world coal reserves by leading countries is shown in Fig. 1.2.

**Table 1.2:** Coal reserves of top 10 countries

| Country | Coal Reserves (Million Tonnes) | % Share of global coal reserves |
|---|---|---|
| U. S | 248,941 | 23% |
| Russia | 162,166 | 15% |
| Australia | 150,227 | 14% |
| China | 143,197 | 13% |
| India | 111,052 | 10% |
| Germany | 35,900 | 3% |
| Indonesia | 34,869 | 3% |
| Ukraine | 34,375 | 3% |
| Poland | 28,395 | 2% |
| Kazakhstan | 25,605 | 2% |

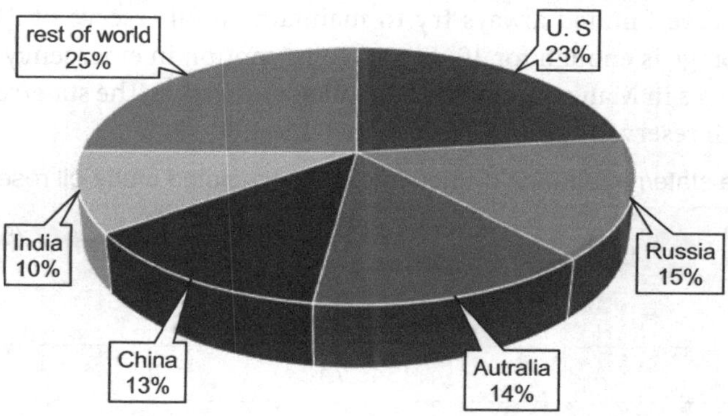


**Fig. 1.2:** World coal reserves in year 2021
(**Source:** BP statistical review of world energy 2021).

It is to be noted that the first five countries (U.S., Russia, Australia, China and India) have 75% of global coal reserves and rest of the world have 25%.

## 1.3.2 Oil Reserves

Oil, also known as petroleum, is a fossil fuel. It is a naturally occurring liquid fuel, yellowish-black in colour. It is mainly the mixtures of different hydrocarbons. Oil is formed naturally when huge amount of dead organisms deep inside the earth are subjected to high temperature and pressure for a long duration. Crude oil is extracted from the Oil well by Drilling. Oil Wells are constructed by boring in the earth at specific sites identified by the geological survey. The "oil reserve" is the amount of crude oil located in a particular economic region and can be reasonably extracted from the earth. This extraction must be technically viable and financially feasible with respect to the current price of oil. Oil is considered as the principal source of fuel and one of the main overall sources of the primary energy. According to U.S. Energy Information Administration (EIA) 2022, world uses around 92.2-million-barrel oil per day which is about 30% of global overall primary energy use.

For oil reserves, world can be categorised in two group of countries:

(i) OPEC (the Organization of PetroleumExporting Countries) member countries

(ii) Non-OPEC member countries: Countries which are not the member of OPEC

The organization of petroleum exporting countries (OPEC) is an inter-governmental organization of 13 member countries. It was founded on September 14, 1960 with 5 initial member countries in Baghdad, Iraq. The five initial members were Iran, Iraq, Kuwait, Saudi Arabia and Venezuela. At present, 13 countries namely Algeria, Angola, Congo, Equatorial Guinea, Gabon,Iran, Iraq, Kuwait, Libya, Nigeria, Saudi Arabia, the United Arab Emirates and Venezuela have become the members of OPEC.

### 1.3.2.1 India's Oil Reserves

The first oil deposit in India was discovered in 1889 in Digboi town in Tinsukia district of Assam. The current crude oil reserves in India isestimated about 4963.98million barrels. India's most of the crude oil reserves are found in the western offshore (39.6%) and in Assam (26.48%). The percentage share of the state/region is presented as chart in Fig. 1.3. Having oil reserves in the form of underground storage, above the ground storage and fully developed reserves where oil extraction can be done easily is a profitable idea for the country like India which is basically an oil-importing country. The Indian Strategic Petroleum Reserve Limited always try to maintain an oil reserve of 31.5 million barrels. At present this strategic storage is enough for 10 days of consumption in emergency situation. Strategic oil storage is located at 3 places in Mangalore, Visakhapatnam and Padur. The state/region wise distribution of the estimated crude oil reserves in India in given in Table 1.3.

**Table 1.3:** The state/region wise distribution of the estimated crude oil reserves in India

| State/Region | Crude Oil Reserves (million barrels) | % Share of Oil |
|---|---|---|
| Western offshore | 2021.24 | 39.6 |
| Assam | 1345.74 | 26.48 |
| Gujarat | 1002.25 | 19.63 |
| Eastern Offshore | 343.66 | 6.73 |
| Rajasthan | 207.45 | 4.06 |
| Tamil Nadu | 76.05 | 1.49 |
| Andhra Pradesh | 68.86 | 1.35 |
| Nagaland | 20.11 | 0.39 |
| Arunachal Pradesh | 12.84 | 0.25 |

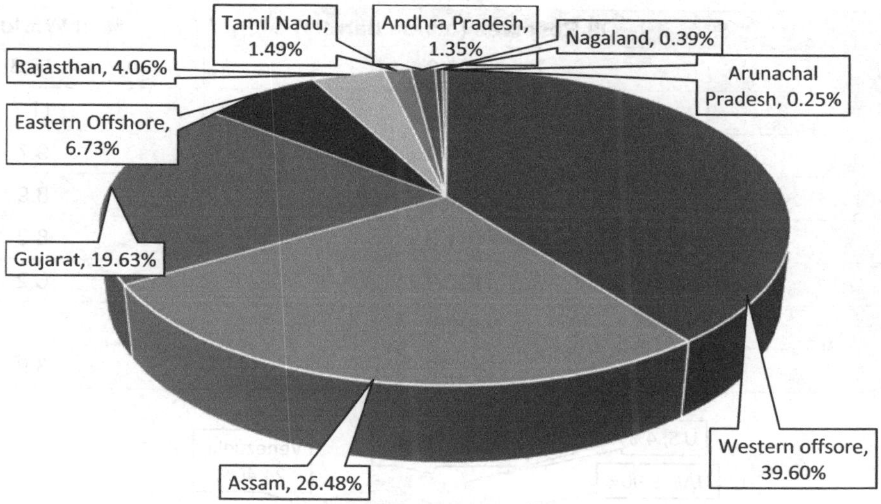


**Fig. 1.3:** Percentage share of states/region in India's Oil reserve

### *1.3.2.2 World Oil Reserves*

As per the current estimate, OPEC member countries have 1241.82 billion barrels of oil reserves which is around 80% of the total global crude oil reserves. Of the total oil reserved by OPEC, most of the oil is reserved by the middle east countries. This share is around 67% of the OPEC total oil reserves. The non-OPEC countries have oil reserves of 303.25 billion barrels which is about 20 % of the total reserves. The percentage share the oil reserves by OPEC and non-OPEC member countries is shown in Fig. 1.4.

The amount of oil reserve and its percentage share of total oil reserves by top 10 leading countries are listed in the Table 1.4 and in Fig. 1.5 respectively. Venezuela has the largest oil reserves of 303.47 billion barrels with percentage share of 24.4 %. Despite of the fact that Venezuela has the most share of the Oil reserves, majority of its oil reserves are offshore and deep in the ground. The oil extraction by using current technology is not profitable. The extraction in Saudi Arabia's oil reserves on the other hand is comparatively easier and economical because the oil reserves are close to the surface which makes Saudi Arabia's oil sector more fruitful and profit making.

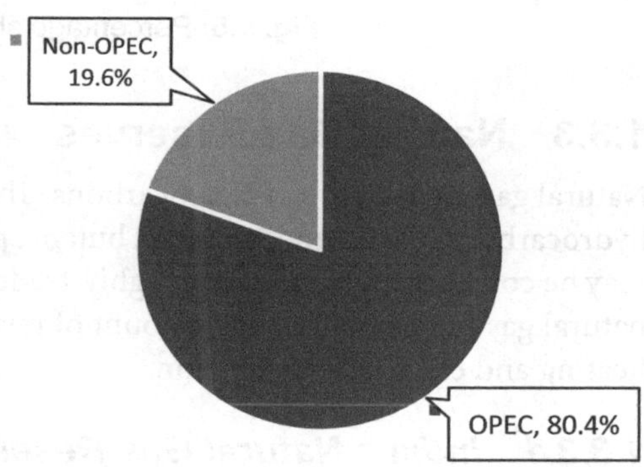


**Fig. 1.4:** Oil reserves of OPEC andnon-OPEC

**Table 1.4:** Leading countries in Oil reserves

| Country | Oil Reserves (billion barrels) | % of World total |
|---|---|---|
| Venezuela | 303.47 | 24.4 |
| Saudi Arabia | 267.19 | 21.5 |

| Country | Oil Reserves (billion barrels) | % of World total |
|---|---|---|
| Iran | 208.6 | 16.8 |
| Iraq | 145.02 | 11.7 |
| Canada | 168.1 | 9.7 |
| UAE | 111 | 8.9 |
| Kuwait | 101.5 | 8.2 |
| Russia | 107.8 | 6.2 |
| U S | 68.8 | 4 |
| Libya | 48.36 | 3.9 |

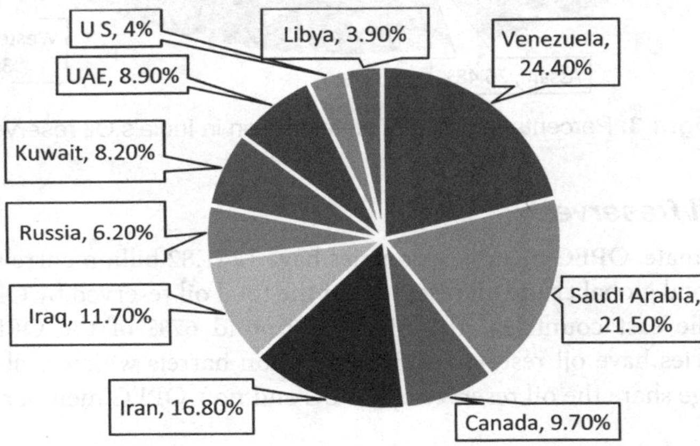


**Fig. 1.5:** Percentage share of top 10 countries in Oil reserves

## 1.3.3 Natural Gas Reserves

Natural gas is a mixture of hydrocarbons. The main constituent is methane with small fractions of other hydrocarbons like ethane, propane, butane, pentane, octane and other higher hydrocarbons. Natural gas may be considered as one of the highly-traded asset of any country. The country having large reserves of natural gas can generate huge amount of revenue by exporting it. Natural gas is mostly used in cooking, heating and electricity generation.

### *1.3.3.1 India's Natural Gas Reserves*

The estimated natural gas reserves in India were about 48.47 trillion cubic feet. This reserve was only 25.8 trillion cubic feet in the year 2000. This shows that there was about 80% of growth in gas reserves in 20 years. India is on the 22nd place in the world with the share of 0.7% of the world's total natural gas reserves. At current consumption rate India is left with 22 years of natural gas. In India natural gas is found in both eastern and western parts of India. In western part most of the gas reserves are located in Barmer area in Rajasthan, Gulf of Kutch and Gulf of Khanbat in Gujarat, Bassein and Bombay high region in Maharashtra. In the eastern India, most of the gas reserves are found in Assam. Natural gas fields are also found in some region of Tripura, on the coast of Odisha, Krishna-Godavari basin of

Andhra Pradesh and Cauvery basin of Tamil Nadu. The percentage share of states and regions in India has been represented by chart in Fig. 1.6. In the eastern offshore the oil reserves are 40.6% and in the western offshore it is around 23.7%.

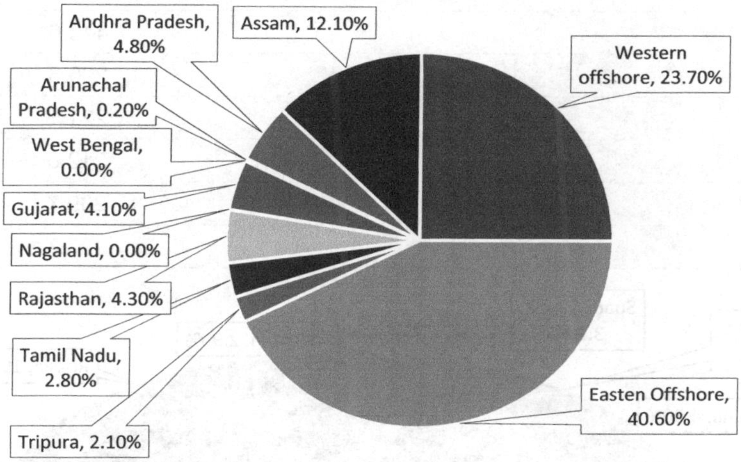


**Fig. 1.6:** Percentage share of countries in global natural gas reserves
(**Source:** BP statistical Review of World Energy, 2021 and EIA)

### *1.3.3.2 World's Natural Gas Reserves*

The total world proven gas reserve was about 7257 trillion cubic feet as of January 01, 2020. As per the data reported by U S Energy Information Administration (EIA), in the start of year 2021 most of the proven gas reserve was found in Russia, Iran and Qatar followed by United States of America and Saudi Arabia. Russia has proven gas reserve of about 1320.5 trillion cubic feet which is around 20% of the total world's total gas reserves. Most of the Russia's reserves are located in the Siberia region. Iran is on the second position in terms of gas reserves. It has around 1133.6 trillion cubic feet with a share of 17%. With 872 trillion cubic feet of gas reserves, Qatar holds the third position. The percentage share of Qatar is 13% of the world's total. Turkmenistan is on fourth position with 480.3 trillion cubic feet oil reserves with percentage world share of around 7.2 %. Majority of the oil reserves in Turkmenistan is located in Amu Darya basin of southeast, Murgab basin in south and South Caspian basin in the western part of the country. Fifth largest reserve is with the United States of America. It has around 445.6 trillion cubic feet of oil reserve with a percentage share of around 6.7 % of global reserve. Most of the oil reserves in US are located in Texas, Oklahoma and Louisiana.

Saudi Arabia has 212 trillion cubic feet with percentage share of 3.2%. Almost half of the oil reserves in Saudi Arabia are located in the Ghawar on shore field and offshore fields of Safaniya and Zuluf. Top 10 leading countries in natural gas reserves are presented in Table 1.5 and the percentage shares of the world's total reserves by these countries are shown as chart in Fig. 1.7.

**Table 1.5:** World's leading countries in natural gas reserves

| Country | Oil Reserves (trillioncubic feet) |
|---|---|
| Russia | 1320.5 |
| Iran | 1133.6 |

| Country | Oil Reserves (trillioncubic feet) |
|---|---|
| Qatar | 871.5 |
| Turkmenistan | 480.3 |
| United States | 445.6 |
| China | 296.6 |
| Venezuela | 221.1 |
| Suadi Arabia | 212.6 |
| UAE | 209.7 |
| Nigeria | 193.3 |

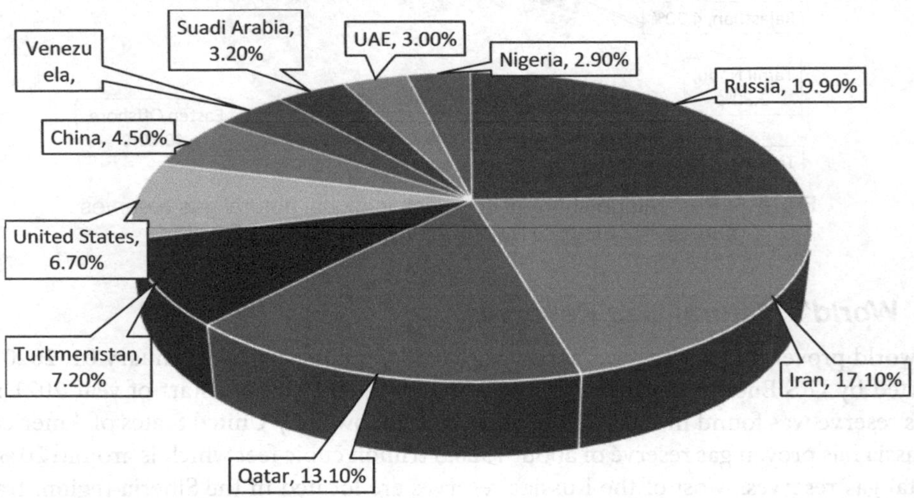


**Fig. 1.7:** Percentage share of countries in global natural gas reserves
**(Source:** statistical Review of World Energy, 2021 and EIA)

## 1.4 WORLD ENERGY SCENARIO

We use energy in the form of fire wood, fossil fuels (coal, oil, and natural gas) and electricity to make our life comfortable.

### 1.4.1 World Energy Consumption

The total energy consumed by any country is decided by many factors like the industrial development, Infrastructure such as roads and electrical grids, living standard of human beings and geographical size of the country. But the most dominant factor for energy consumption is the population of the country. Because of this reason China, India and U.S consume most of the energy produced globally. The countries like British Virgin Islands, Tongo, Dominica, Saint Pierre and Miquelon consume very little energy because of their small population. Countries with most consumption of electricity, oil and total energy are listed below in Table 1.6.

Global primary energy consumption for the year 2021 was 163709 TWh. The fossil fuel consumption was the largest with a share about 83% of the total global energy use. In fossil fuel, the Oil consumption was followed by coal and gas. The source wise use of various types of energy are given in Table 1.7. The source wise energy consumption for the year of 2021 is represented as chart in Fig. 1.8.

**Table 1.6:** Top countries with mass consumption of electricity, oil and total energy

| Country | Electricity consumption (billion kWh) | Oil Consumption (million barrels per day) | Total Energy Consumption (billion kWh) |
|---|---|---|---|
| China | 6875 | 20543 | 145.46 |
| U. S | 3989 | 14008 | 87.79 |
| India | 1229 | 4920 | 31.98 |
| Russia | 943 | 3699 | 28.31 |
| Japan | 904 | 3739 | 17.03 |
| Canada | 553 | 2303 | 13.63 |
| Germany | 517 | 2346 | 12.11 |
| Brazil | 534 | 3142 | 12.01 |

**Table 1.7:** Source wise Consumption

| Energy Source | Consumption (TWh) | Energy Source | Consumption (TWh) |
|---|---|---|---|
| Oil | 51170 | Wind | 4872 |
| Coal | 44473 | Solar | 2702 |
| Gas | 40375 | Biofuels | 1140 |
| Nuclear | 7031 | Other Renewables | 763 |
| Hydropower | 11183 | **TOTAL** | **163709 TWh** |

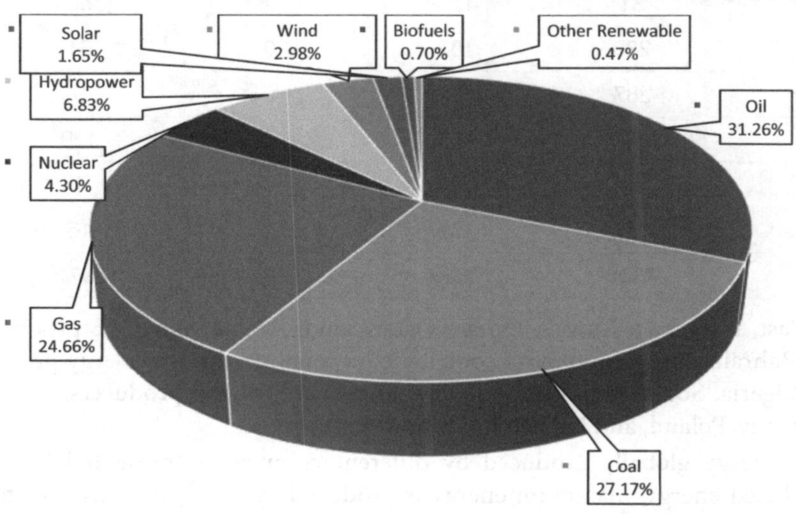


**Fig. 1.8:** Source wise energy consumption for the year of 2021.
(**Source:** BP Statistical Review of World Energy, 2022)

### 1.4.2 Energy Production

The energy production may be considered as one of the basic parts of the economic activities of any country. The energy generation capacity and its use isgenerally taken as one of the important parameters for the economic, social and industrial development of the country. The process of energy production which is directly extracted or captured from the natural resources is known as primary energy production.

The production of energy from different resources can be categorised as:

(i) Energy produced from Fossil fuels like Coal, Oil and Natural Gases.

(ii) Energy produced from Nuclear Power.

(iii) Energy produced from renewable energy resources like Solar, Wind, Biomass, Hydropower, geothermal, tidal, wave etc.

The countries and regions which produce about 90% of the globally produced primary energy are listed below in Table 1.8

**Table 1.8:** Leading producers of primary energy

| Country/ Region | Coal (MT) | Oil and Gas (MT) | Nuclear (MT) | Renewable (MT) | Total (MT) |
|---|---|---|---|---|---|
| China | 1860 | 325 | 77 | 300 | 2560 |
| U. S | 369 | 1400 | 219 | 180 | 2170 |
| Middle East | 1 | 2030 | 2 | 4 | 2040 |
| Russia | 240 | 1165 | 54 | 25 | 1484 |
| Africa | 157 | 611 | 3 | 397 | 1169 |
| Europe | 171 | 398 | 244 | 396 | 1111 |
| India | 289 | 67 | 10 | 208 | 574 |
| Canada | 31 | 422 | 26 | 50 | 529 |
| Indonesia | 288 | 102 | 0 | 61 | 451 |
| Australia | 287 | 115 | 0 | 9 | 412 |
| Brazil | 2 | 160 | 4 | 129 | 296 |
| Kazakhstan | 49 | 128 | 0 | 1 | 159 |
| Mexico | 7 | 132 | 4 | 16 | 159 |
| **World** | **3890** | **7850** | **707** | **1972** | **14420** |

In Middle East, Iran, Iraq, Kuwait, Oman, Qatar, Saudi Arabia, and UAE produced most of the Energy whereas Bahrain, Jordan and Syria contributed a small part of the energy produced in Middle East. In Africa: Nigeria, South Africa, Algeria and Angola are the top producers. In Europe: Norway, France, UK, Germany, Poland, and Netherland produced the most.

Source wise energy globally produced by different countries is presented in Fig. 1.9. Of the world's total produced energy, maximum energy is produced by coal (10042.2TWh) followed by Gas (6098.05TWh) and then by Hydropower (4206.14TWh).

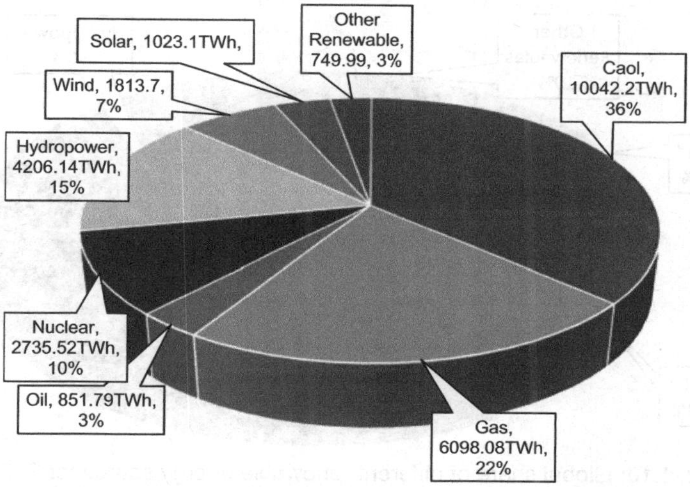


**Fig.1.9:** Source wise world energy production in 2021
(**Source:** BP Statistical Review of World Energy, Ember Global Electricity Review (2022) & Ember European Electricity Review (2022))

## 1.5 RENEWABLE ENERGY SCENARIO

Because of the day by day increase in population, industrial and economic development, the energy consumption around the world is increasing at a very rapid rate.Presently, to fulfil the energy demand, conventional energy sources like coal, oil and natural gas is being used to large extent. The number of global reserves of the fossil fuels is decreasing with very fast rate and may be depleted in few hundreds of years. The energy consumption is increasing; supply is decreasing, thus resulting in energy shortage. This is known as energy crisis. Alternative or renewable energy sources like Solar, Wind, Geothermal, Biomass, Tidal, Wave etc. are becoming essential to develop for future energy use. Use of renewable energy resources has gained momentum in the past decades because energy can be produced again and again by these resources. It is clean, safe, environmentally friendly and more sustainable. Renewable energy sources havea huge potential as theycan fulfil or supplementthe world's growing energy demand.

### 1.5.1 World's Renewable Energy Scenario

The use of energy based on the renewable energy sources is greatly increasing around the world. A transformation is observed from conventional energy use toward renewable energy. In recent years the growth rate in the renewable energy market is higher as compared with the growth rate in the conventional fuel market.The share of renewable energy to the total global energy was about 8.6 % with 437GW installed capacity in the year 2010. It was increased by more than 2.5 times in 2017 and reached to 1236 GW with share of 18.2 % of total installed capacity. It was further increased by 22.5% in year 2020 and reported as 2802 GW. It was increased to 3064 gigawatts in 2021. The largest share in the total was of hydropower in 2021. Hydropower generation capacity was 1230 GW with percentage share of about 58%. Wind and Solar accounted for 21% and 11% share, respectively. The share of other renewable sources which includes geothermal, bioenergy, waste, tidal and wave energy was about 10% to the total renewable energy installed capacity. The percentage share of different renewable energy source is presented in Fig. 1.10 for year 2021.

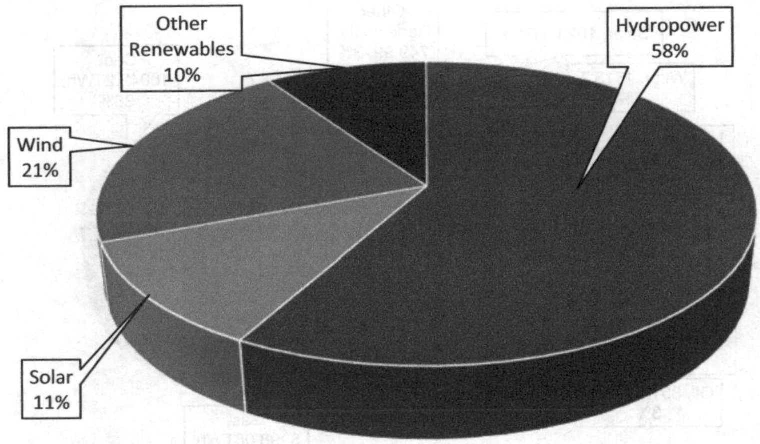


**Fig. 1.10:** Global share of different renewable energy source for 2021
(**Source:** BP statistical Review of World Energy, 2021 and EIA)

China followed by U.S and Brazil were the three leading countries with maximum share to the total installed renewable energy capacity in 2021. China was on the first place with installed capacity of around 1020 GW. U.S was on the second position with installed capacity of 325 GW and Brazil on the third position with installed capacity of around 160 GW. The top 10 countries with their installed capacities are listed in Table 1.9.

**Table 1.9:** World's leading countries in Renewable energy installed capacity

| Country | Renewable Energy Installed capacity for 2021 (GW) |
|---|---|
| China | 1020 |
| US | 325 |
| Brazil | 160 |
| India | 147 |
| Germany | 138 |
| Japan | 112 |
| Canada | 103 |
| France | 60 |
| Italy | 57 |
| Russia | 56 |

## 1.5.2 India's Renewable Energy Scenario

India also has a great potential in renewable energy which is estimated around 1000 GW. Renewable energy has a share of 26.53% in the total installed capacity in the country. India is on the third position in renewable energy country index 2021 and ranked fourth for total installed renewable energy capacitywith installed capacity of around 159.95 GW as on 31th March 2022. India's installed renewable energy capacity has increased by 396% in the last 8.5 years.India has set a goal to achieve renewable energy installed capacity of 175 GW with 100 GW of Solar, 60 GW of Wind, 10 GW of Biopower by end of 2022. As of March 2022, the total renewable energy installed capacity in India was 159.95 GW. The largest share is of the wind energy with 40.08 GW. The shares of Solar and other renewable energy resources are as follows:

- Solar Power: 56.6 GW
- Biopower: 11.93 GW
- Small Hydro Power: 4.83 GW
- Large Hydro Power: 46.51

The generation capacity of conventional and renewable energy sources and their percentage to total generation for the years 2015-2016, 2016-2017, 2017-2018, 12018-19, 2019-20 and 2020-21 has been listed in Table 1.10.

The source wise energy generation from renewable energy sources for year 2020-21 is presented by Chart given in Fig. 1.11.

**Table 1.10:** generation capacity for conventional and renewable energy sources and their percentage

| Years | Generation capacity from conventional sources (MU) | Generation capacity form RES (MU) | Toral Generation capacity (MU) | % of RES w.r.t total generation |
|---|---|---|---|---|
| 2015-16 | 1107822.28 | 65780.86 | 1173603.14 | 5.61 |
| 2016-17 | 1160140.90 | 1548.21 | 1241689.11 | 6.57 |
| 2017-18 | 1206306.20 | 101839.48 | 1308145.68 | 7.79 |
| 2018-19 | 1249340.00 | 126760.00 | 1376100.00 | 9.21 |
| 2019-20 | 1250783.91 | 138337.02 | 1389120.93 | 9.95 |
| 2020-21 | 1234607.64 | 147247.51 | 1381855.15 | 10.66 |

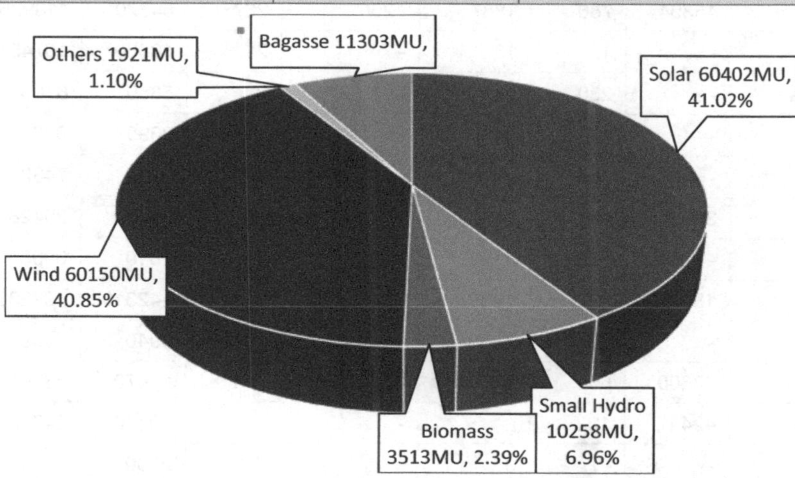


**Fig. 1.11:** Share of different renewable energy source in India for 2021
(**Source:** BP statistical Review of World Energy, 2021 and EIA)

As per the data reported by MNRE (Ministry of New and Renewable Energy Resources) in 2019 the state wise and source wise renewable energy potential in India is given in Table 1.11.

**Table 1.11:** State wise and source wise renewable energy potential in India

| Sl. No. | States/ UTs | Wind Power @ 100m | Small Hydro Power | Biomass Power | Co-generation-bagasse | Waste to Energy | Solar Energy | Total | Distribution (%) |
|---|---|---|---|---|---|---|---|---|---|
| 1 | Andhra Pradesh | 44229 | 409 | 578 | 300 | 123 | 38440 | 84079 | 7.66 |
| 2 | Arunachal Pradesh | - | 2065 | 8 | - | - | 8650 | 10723 | 0.98 |
| 3 | Assam | - | 202 | 212 | - | 8 | 13760 | 14182 | 1.29 |
| 4 | Bihar | - | 527 | 619 | 300 | 73 | 11200 | 12719 | 1.16 |
| 5 | Chhattisgarh | 77 | 1098 | 236 | - | 24 | 18270 | 19705 | 1.80 |
| 6 | Goa | 1 | 5 | 26 | - | - | 880 | 911 | 0.08 |
| 7 | Gujarat | 84431 | 202 | 1221 | 350 | 112 | 35770 | 122086 | 11.12 |
| 8 | Haryana | - | 107 | 1333 | 350 | 24 | 4560 | 6374 | 0.58 |
| 9 | Himachal Pradesh | - | 3460 | 142 | - | 2 | 33840 | 37444 | 3.41 |
| 10 | Jammu & Kashmir | - | 1707 | 43 | - | - | 111050 | 112800 | 10.28 |
| 11 | Jharkhand | - | 228 | 90 | - | 10 | 18180 | 18508 | 1.69 |
| 12 | Karnataka | 55857 | 3726 | 1131 | 450 | - | 24700 | 85864 | 7.82 |
| 13 | Kerala | 1700 | 647 | 1044 | - | 36 | 6110 | 9538 | 0.87 |
| 14 | Madhya Pradesh | 10484 | 820 | 1364 | - | 78 | 61660 | 74406 | 6.78 |
| 15 | Maharashtra | 45394 | 786 | 1887 | 1250 | 287 | 64320 | 113925 | 10.38 |
| 16 | Manipur | - | 100 | 13 | - | 2 | 10630 | 10745 | 0.98 |
| 17 | Meghalaya | - | 230 | 11 | - | 2 | 5860 | 6103 | 0.56 |
| 18 | Mizoram | - | 169 | 1 | - | 2 | 9090 | 9261 | 0.84 |
| 19 | Nagaland | - | 182 | 10 | - | - | 7290 | 7482 | 0.68 |
| 20 | Odisha | 3093 | 286 | 246 | - | 22 | 25780 | 29428 | 2.68 |
| 21 | Punjab | - | 578 | 3172 | 300 | 45 | 2810 | 6905 | 0.63 |
| 22 | Rajasthan | 18770 | 52 | 1039 | - | 62 | 142310 | 162233 | 14.78 |
| 23 | Sikkim | - | 267 | 2 | - | - | 4940 | 5209 | 0.47 |
| 24 | Tamil Nadu | 33800 | 604 | 1070 | 450 | 151 | 17670 | 53745 | 4.90 |
| 25 | Telangana | 4244 | 102 |  | - | - | 20410 | 24756 | 2.26 |
| 26 | Tripura | - | 47 | 3 | - | 2 | 2080 | 2131 | 0.19 |
| 27 | Uttar Pradesh | - | 461 | 1617 | 1250 | 176 | 22830 | 26333 | 2.40 |
| 28 | Uttarakhand | - | 1664 | 24 | - | 5 | 16800 | 18493 | 1.69 |
| 29 | West Bengal | 2 | 392 | 396 | - | 148 | 6260 | 7198 | 0.66 |

| Sl. No. | States/ UTs | Wind Power @ 100m | Small Hydro Power | Biomass Power | Co-generation-bagasse | Waste to Energy | Solar Energy | Total | Distribution (%) |
|---|---|---|---|---|---|---|---|---|---|
| 30 | Andaman & Nicobar | 8 | 7 | | - | - | - | 15 | 0.00 |
| 31 | Chandigarh | - | - | - | - | 6 | - | 6 | 0.00 |
| 32 | Dadar & Nagar Haveli | - | - | - | - | - | - | - | - |
| 33 | Daman & Diu | - | - | - | - | - | - | - | - |
| 34 | Delhi | - | - | - | - | 131 | 2050 | 2181 | 0.20 |
| 35 | Lakshadweep | 8 | - | - | - | - | - | 8 | 0.00 |
| 36 | Puducherry | 153 | - | - | - | 3 | - | 156 | 0.01 |
| 37 | Others (Industrial waste) | - | - | - | - | 1022 | 790 | 1812 | 0.17 |
| | India Total | 302251 | 21134 | 17536 | 5000 | 2554 | 748990 | 1097465 | 100.00 |
| | Distribution (%) | 27.54 | 1.93 | 1.60 | 0.46 | 0.23 | 68.25 | 100.00 | |

## 1.6 ENERGY AND ENVIRONMENT

Now a day's energy has become one of the major needs of the modern society.The environmental problems like air pollution, water pollution, climate change, global warming etc. are directly related with the energy production and its consumption.The energy can be produced by using conventional energy resources like coal, oil, natural gas etc. and also by renewable energy resources like solar, wind, biomass etc. Different types of energy resources have different impact on the environment.

### 1.6.1 Impact of Conventional Energy on Environment

Use of fossil fuel is powering the industrial development and the amenities of the modern society that we are enjoying since long time.In today's world most of our energy requirement is being fulfilled by the burning of fossil fuels like Coal, Oil and natural gas. Because of the burning of fossil fuels, the chemicals and hazardous emissions are released in the atmosphere which are not only polluting the environment but are also deteriorating the health conditions of the human being living on the planetearth. Some examples of such chemicals are carbon mono oxide (CO), carbon dioxide ($CO_2$), Nitrogen oxides ($NO_x$) and Sulphur di-oxides ($SO_2$) etc. These emitted pollutants are the main reason for the smog, acid rain, global warming and climate change like environmentalproblems. At present, these environmental problems have reached such a high level that it becomes a serious threat for the growth of vegetables, wild life and human health. Air pollution causes the depletion of the ozone layer of the atmosphere which leads to climate change.

### 1.6.2 Impact of Renewable Energy on Environment

The environmental problems can be reduced by replacing the conventional energy resources with renewable energy resources like Solar, Wind, Hydropower, Biopower, Wave, Tidal etc.These sources are considered environmentally friendly as theyemit no or very little hazardous and poisonous gases. The trend suggests that renewable energy is going to become an important source of power generation in near future. The major renewable energy sources with their use are given in Table 1.12.

**Table 1.12:** Renewable energy sources with their use

| Renewable energy resource | Energy conversion and uses |
|---|---|
| Solar | Solar home systems, solar water heater, solar dryers, photovoltaics, thermal power generation solar cookers, green house |
| Wind | Power generation, wind mills, wind generations |
| Hydropower | Power generation |
| Geothermal | Urban heating, power generation, hydrothermal, hot rocks |
| Biomass | Heat and power generation, pyrolysis, gasification, digestion |
| Wave | Numerous designs |
| Tidal | Barrage, tidal stream |

Air pollution and greenhouse gas emissions can be minimised by making the proper use of renewable energy resources. The various impacts of renewable energy on environments are presented in Table 1.13.

**Table 1.13:** Effect of renewable energy sources on environment

| Category of Impact | Comparison with conventional sources | Comments |
|---|---|---|
| Emission of Hg, Cd and other toxic elements | Reduces emission | Emission reduced a few hundred times |
| Emission of particles | Reduces emission | Much less emission. |
| $CO_2$ emissions | Reduces emission | A big advantage. |
| Acid rain, SO, NOx | Reduces emission | Reduced more than 25 times. |
| Other greenhouse gases | Reduces greenhouse gases | Big advantage-global warming |
| Water quality | Better quality water | Reduced water pollution. |
| Soil erosion | Smaller loss of land | In most cases, there is no penetration deep in the earth |

## 1.7 ECONOMICS OF RENEWABLE ENERGY SYSTEMS

It has been observed that renewable energy systems have advantages over the systems based on conventional energy sources in terms of economics. The two main reasons why renewable energy systems are economical are (1) They generally utilize local materials (2) local labour from villages and rural area. They create more jobs and greater earnings than conventional electricity generation systems. The renewable energy industry provides variety of jobs from high-tech photovoltaic module manufacturing to maintenance jobs at solar and wind power generation sites. In addition to the development of new and appropriate technology, issue related to their financial and economic viability of renewable energy system are being given considerable importance. Techno-economic analysis is the area of engineering where engineering judgment and experience are utilized. Analysis is used for project cost control, profitability analysis, planning, scheduling and optimization of operational research etc. In the case of renewable energy systems, it is necessary to work out its economic viability so that the users may know the importance and they can utilize the area under their command for best output from renewable energy systems.

### 1.7.1 Levelized Cost of Electricity (LCOE)

The economic analysis of renewable energy system includes the initial cost of components, cost of operation,including maintenance, labour and other costs. The price of the electricity per kWh is also considered in the economic analysis. Various methods are available now a days for electricity generation like coal based thermal power plants, wind turbines, gas-turbines, fuels cells, solar thermal, solar PV, hydropower etc. For comparing the economics of these different technologies, a method is required which consider the role of both the initial costs and running (operational) cost of the system. One of such matrices commonly accepted by industries is known as Levelized Cost of Energy (LCOE).

The LCOE can be calculated as:

$$LCOE = \frac{Sum\,of\,total\,costs\,over\,ligetime}{Sum\,of\,elctricity\,produced\,over\,lifetime} = \frac{\sum_{t=1}^{n}\frac{I_t+M_t+F_t}{(1+r)^t}}{\sum_{t=1}^{n}\frac{E_t}{(1+r)^t}}$$

Where,

$I_t$ is the Investment cost in year t

$M_t$ is the operation and maintenance cost in year t

$F_t$ is the fuel cost in the year t (if any)

$E_t$ is the electricity generated in year t

r is the discount rate

n is the expected lifetime of the system

LCOE represents the average revenue per unit of electricity generated and is given in currency per kilowatt hour(Rs. per kWh or EUR per kWh or USD per kWh etc.).It does not represent the electricity for users and is important for the power generation companies.

**Example for calculation of LCOE:** Let us consider a wind energy plant which takes one year to complete. The initial investment cost is $ 1500. The operation and Maintenance (O&M) costs are $ 100 per year. The growth rate is 2% and no fuel is used. The plant life time is 10 years. The discount rate is 8%. The calculation for LCOE is presented here.

| Initial Investment Cost ($): | 1500 |
|---|---|
| Operation and Maintenance Cost ($): | 100 per year |
| O & M Growth rate (%): | 2 % |
| Annual Fuel Cost ($): | 0 |
| Annual Electricity output (kWh): | 3000 |
| System Life (Yr): | 10 |
| Discount Rate (%): | 8% |

| Total Costs | Entry | 1 | 2 | 3 | 4 | 5 | 6 | 7 | 8 | 9 | 10 |
|---|---|---|---|---|---|---|---|---|---|---|---|
| Initial Investment ($) | 1500 | | | | | | | | | | |

| O & M Costs | | - | 100 | 102 | 104 | 106 | 108 | 110 | 113 | 115 | 117 |
|---|---|---|---|---|---|---|---|---|---|---|---|
| Fuel Costs | | - | - | - | - | - | - | - | - | - | - |
| Discount Factor | | 92.6 % | 85.7 % | 79.4 % | 73.5 % | 68.1 % | 63 % | 58.3 % | 54 % | 50 % | 46.3 % |
| Present value of cost ($) | 1500 | | 86 | 81 | 76 | 72 | 68 | 64 | 61 | 57 | 54 |
| **Sum of Total costs over lifetime ($)** | **$ 2121** | | | | | | | | | | |
| **Energy Output** | **Entry** | **1** | **2** | **3** | **4** | **5** | **6** | **7** | **8** | **9** | **10** |
| Yearly Output | | | 3000 | 3000 | 3000 | 3000 | 3000 | 3000 | 3000 | 3000 | 3000 |
| Discount Factor | | 92.6 % | 85.7 % | 79.4 % | 73.5 % | 68.1 % | 63 % | 58.3 % | 54 % | 50 % | 46.3 % |
| Present value (kWh) | | | 2572 | 2381 | 2205 | 2042 | 1891 | 1750 | 1621 | 1501 | 1390 |
| **Sum of total electricity produced over lifetime (kWh)** | **17352kWh** | | | | | | | | | | |
| **LCOE = $2121/17352 kWh = $0.12/kWh** | | | | | | | | | | | |

## UNIT SUMMARY

- Energy measures the ability to do work.
- Unit of energy is Joule (J), Watt-hour (Wh), Kilowatt-hour (kWh), Tetra Watt-hour (TWh) etc.
- Energy is an important parameter for the industrial, economic and social development of any country.
- Energy utilization one of the deciding parametersfor degree of development of a country.
- Conventional energy resources like coal, Oil and natural gas are limited in stock and causes pollution.
- Renewable energy sources like solar, wind, biomass, geothermal, wave energy, tidal energy etc. are available is unlimited stock in nature and are nearly pollution free.
- Of the world'stotal produced energy, maximum is produced by coal (10042.2TWh) followed by Gas (6098.05TWh) and Hydropower (4206.14TWh).
- In terms of the total world energy consumption, China consumed most of the energy (145.46 billion kilowatt-hour) followed by United States of America.
- India is on the third position in terms of overallglobal energy consumption.
- The fossil fuel consumption was the largest with a share about 83% of the total global energy use.
- Coal is one of the largest and primary sources of commercial energy worldwide.

- Anthracite comes in the highest rank of the coal. In India, Anthracite deposits are located in Kashmir and Eastern Himalayas region.
- The first five countries (U.S, Russia, Australia, China and India) have 75% of global coal reserves and rest of the world have 25%.
- India is the second highest coal producing country in the world and fifth world's largest country in terms of coal deposits. India is production about 783 million tonnes of coal.
- Jharkhand has the most coal reserves in India followed by Odisha and Chhattisgarh.
- According to U.S. Energy Information Administration (EIA) 2022, world uses around 92.2-million-barrel oil per day which is about 30% of global overall primary energy use.
- The organization of petroleum exporting countries (OPEC) is an intergovernmental organization of 13 member countries.
- OPEC member countries have share of around 67% to the total oil reserves.
- Venezuela has the largest oil reserves of 303.47 billion barrels with percentage share of 24.4 %.
- The first oil deposit in India was discovered in 1889 in Digboi town in Tinsukia district of Assam.
- India's most of the crude oil reserves is found in the western offshore (39.6%) and in Assam (26.48%).
- In the start of year 2021 most of the proven gas reserve was found in Russia, Iran and Qatar followed by United States of America and Saudi Arabia.
- As of 2021 the total global installed renewable energy capacity in 3064 gigawatts.
- Hydropower generation capacity is 1230 GW with percentage share of about 58% to global total.
- China followed by U.S and Brazil were the three leading countries with maximum share to the total installed renewable energy capacity in 2021.
- India is on fourth position in terms of renewable energy installed capacity with percentage share of 26.53 % of world's total.
- As of March 2022, the total renewable energy installed capacity in India was 159.95 GW. The largest share is of wind energy with 40.08 GW.
- The environmental problems like air pollution, water pollution, climate change, global warming etc are directly related with the energy production and its consumption.
- The pollutants emitted by conventional energy resources are the main reason for the smog, acid rain, global warming and climate change like environmental problems.
- The environmental problems can be reduced by replacing the conventional energy resources by renewable energy resources like Solar, Wind, Hydropower, Biopower, Wave, Tidal etc.
- Renewable energy systems have advantages over the systems based on conventional energy sources in terms of economics.
- LCOE (Levelized cost of electricity or energy) is a matrix which represents the average revenue per unit of electricity generated and is given in currency per kilowatt hour (Rs. per kWh or EUR per kWh or USD per kWh etc.).

# EXERCISES

## Multiple Choice Questions

1. Energy measures
   (a) the ability to do work (b) the rate of displacement
   (b) the time of displacement (d) the rate of force applied
2. Which is not a Renewable Source of Energy
   (a) Solar (b) Oil
   (c) Wind (d) Hydropower
3. The Unit of Energy is
   (a) Joule (b) TWh
   (c) kWh (d) All of these
4. In terms of total primary energy consumption, India stands
   (a) first (b) second
   (c) third (d) fifth
5. Where is the largest coal belt in India?
   (a) Uttar Pradesh (b) Jharkhand
   (c) Assam (d) Kerala
6. At present the first two leading countries in Oil reserves are
   (a) Iran and Iraq
   (b) Venezuela and Saudi Arabia
   (c) India and China
   (d) U.S and Canada
7. Which form of coalcomes in the highest rank
   (a) Peat (b) Lignites
   (c) Bituminous (d) Anthracite
8. Full for of LCOE is
   (a) life cycle of energy (b) levelized cycle of Energy
   (b) levelized cost of electricity (d) none of these
9. LOCE is represented in
   (a) Rs. per kWh (b) USD per kWh
   (c) EUR per kWh (d) all of these
10. Which one is not emitted in the burning of fossil fuels
    (a) $CO_2$ (b) CO
    (c) $NO_x$ (d) $O_2$
11. Which has the largest share among all renewable energy resource in the World
    (a) wind energy (b) solar energy
    (c) hydropower energy (d) biofuel

12. Which has the largest share in among all renewable energy resource in India
    (a) wind energy (b) solar energy
    (c) hydropower energy (d) biofuel
13. At present number of member countries in OPEC
    (a) 10 (b) 11
    (c) 12 (d) 13
14. Which country is not the member of OPEC
    (a) Russia (a) Kuwait
    (c) UAE (d) Iran
15. Which country has the maximum share to the total installed renewable energy capacity
    (a) India (b) China
    (c) Russia (d) U.S

| Answers of Multiple Choice Questions | | | | | | | |
|---|---|---|---|---|---|---|---|
| 1. (a) | 2. (b) | 3. (d) | 4. (c) | 5. (b) | 6. (b) | 7. (d) | 8. (b) |
| 9. (d) | 10. (d) | 11. (c) | 12. (a) | 13. (d) | 14. (a) | 15. (b) | |

## Short and Long Answer Type Questions

### *Category I*

1. Define renewable energy resources. Give few examples.
2. Explain in brief the impact of conventional energy resources on environment.
3. Define LCOE. How it is beneficial for power generation companies.
4. What is an energy system? Explain in Brief.
5. Explain advantages of use of renewable energy resources.

### *Category II*

1. What is significance of energy? Differentiate between renewable and non-renewable energy resources.
2. Discuss potential of different renewable energy sources in Indian context.
3. Define reserve energy sources. Discuss the status of Coal reserves in India.
4. Discuss the impact of conventional energy use on environment. Show how renewable energy is assumed as environmental friendly.
5. Discuss the global scenario of energy generated by different renewable energy technologies.

## KNOW MORE

Energy resources currently used to fulfil most of our daily energy demand are mostly fossil fuels andnuclear energy. These resources are non-renewable and someday will be exhausted. The other challenge is that with their impact on environment related to air pollution, water pollution, global warming, climate change, land use, waste disposal.

**Global Warming and Climate Change(Greenhouse effect)**

The phenomenon in which the radiative energy leaving the earth surface is absorbed by some atmospheric gases is called greenhouse effect. The gases are called as greenhouse gases. In this process the heat is trapped close to the Earth surface by greenhouse gases. Carbon dioxide ($CO_2$), methane ($CH_4$), nitrous oxide ($NO_x$), hydro-chloro-fluoro-carbons (HCFCs) and Ozone are the main greenhouse gases.Thesegases can be thought of as a blanket wrapped around the Earth, keeping the Earth warm by blocking the heat radiation from the Earth. Carbon dioxide ($CO_2$) is the primary greenhouse gas. The greenhouse effect causes the average temperature of the Earth to rise and the climate generally changes at some locations. These undesirable consequences of the greenhouse effect are generally referred as global warming.

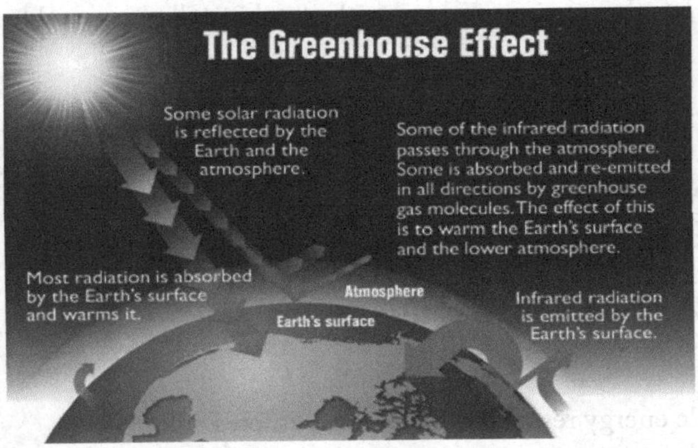


**Fig.** Diagram showing how the greenhouse effect works on Earth

## REFERENCES AND SUGGESTED READINGS


1. J.W. Twidella and A. Weir,*Renewable Energy Sources*, EFN Spon Ltd., UK, 2006.
2. G.N.Tiwariand R.K.Mishra, *Advanced Renewable Energy Resources*, RSC Publishing, UK, 2012.
3. N. H. Ravindranath, U. K. Rao, B. Natarajan, P. Monga,*Renewable Energy andEnvironment-A Policy Analysis for India*, Tata McGraw Hill.
4. R. A. Ristinen and J. J. Kraushaar,*Energy and The Environment, Second Edition*, John Willey & Sons, New York, 2006.
5. D. P. Kothari, *Renewable Energy Sources and Emerging Technologies*, PHI Learning, New Delhi, ISBN: -978-81-203-4470-9

Dynamic QR Code for Further Reading

# 2 Solar PV and Concentrated Solar Power Plants

## UNIT SPECIFICS

In this unit following major points have been discussed:

- Solar radiation spectrum and types of solar radiation
- The availability of solar radiation in various parts of India
- Solar thermal and PV technologies for generating electricity from solar energy
- Different types of concentrating solar plants
- Photovoltaic (PV) cell working and materials used to make solar cells
- ifferent types of PV power generations plants

Wherever possible, examples and block diagrams are used to illustrate the topics. For better practice, we have provided multiple choice questions as well as long and short answer type questions. The unit includes lists of references and suggested readings that can be used for practice. It is important to note that some QR codes have been provided in various sections for getting more information on various topics of interest,which can be scanned for relevant supportive knowledge.

Following the practical section, there is a "Know More" section. This section has been carefully designed so that the supplementary information provided in this section is useful to book users. This section also contains some interesting facts about solar energy use.

## RATIONALE

Solar energy is the most plentiful renewable energy source for power generation. Solar energy can be converted to electrical power using two basic technologies (i) solar thermal technology which uses concentrators to concentrate solar radiation and (ii) Solar photovoltaic technology which converts sunlight directly into electrical power using a device known as a solar cell.

This chapter discusses the solar radiation power available in India as well as the various technologies used to harness solar energy. The operation of photovoltaic cells and various types of solar power plants will be discussed. The chapter also discusses the design and operation of various types of concentrating solar plants (CSP) and PV power plants.

## PRE-REQUISITES

Understanding of the semiconductor physics

## UNIT OUTCOMES

The list of outcomes of this unit is as follows:

**U2-O1:** To study the solar radiation spectrum in India

**U2-O2:** To understand the principle of concentrated solar power

**U2-O3:** To study different types of solar concentrating technology

**U2-O4:** To understand the working of a solar cell

**U2-O5:** To study different types of solar PV power plants

| Unit-2 Outcomes | EXPECTED MAPPING WITH COURSE OUTCOMES (1-Weak Correlation; 2-Medium Correlation; 3-Strong Correlation) | | | | |
|---|---|---|---|---|---|
| | CO-1 | CO-2 | CO-3 | CO-4 | CO-5 |
| U2-O1 | 3 | 2 | - | - | 1 |
| U2-O2 | 3 | - | - | - | - |
| U2-O3 | 3 | - | - | - | - |
| U2-O4 | 3 | - | - | - | - |
| U2-O5 | 3 | - | - | - | 1 |

## 2.1 OVERVIEW

Solar energy is the energy received from the Sun. It is clean, environmentally friendly and infinitely available on the planet.It is a type of renewable energy that allows us to meet some of our energy needs without polluting the environment. Solar photovoltaic (PV) is a field in which sunlight is converted into electrical energy using a device known as a solar cell or photovoltaic (PV) cell. The solar cell is essentially a semiconductor. In solar cells, silicon is the most commonly used semiconductor material. Rapid development has been observed in the photovoltaic field in recent years. Concentrating solar collectors are devices that focus solar radiation in a specific area. These are made up of a series of reflectors or mirrors that focus sunlight on an absorber or receiver. These collectors are used in concentrating solar power (CSP) plants to focus sunlight onto a receiver. Various designs of concentrating solar power plants are available depending on the type of collector.

## 2.2 THE SUN AND ITS ENERGY

The sun is the only star in our solar system, and it is located in the centre. It is the primary source of energy for all life on Earth. The diameter of the sun is 1390000 km which is approximately 109 times the diameter of earth. It has a mass of $1.98 \times 10^{30}$ kg which is approximately 332950 times the mass of earth. The sun accounts for approximately 99.86 per cent of the total mass of the solar system. The photosphere is the sun's visible outer surface. The temperature of this outer surface is around 6000 K. Solar energy is created deep within the sun's core. The sun's enormous energy is released as a result of thermonuclear fusion reaction in the core. Four hydrogen atoms fuse together to form one helium atom in this process. Some mass is converted into energy during this process as per Einstein mass-energy equation $E=\Delta mc^2$, where E is the energy produced, c is the speed of light in a vacuum and $\mathbf{\Delta m}$ is the change in mass or mass defect. This process releases a tremendous amount of energy from the sun. This energy is emitted in all directions but only a small portion of it reaches to earth. Table 2.1 shows the values of various characteristics of the sun.

**Table 2.1:** Values of various characteristics of sun

| Physical Characteristics | |
|---|---|
| Diameter | 1390000 km |
| Mass | 1.98 x $10^{30}$ kg |
| Average density | 1.408 g/$cm^3$ |
| Average surface temperature | 5777 K |
| Volume | 1.41 x $10^{18}$ $km^3$ |
| Age | 4.6 x $10^9$ years |
| **Composition of gases (by mass)** | |
| Hydrogen | 71% |
| Helium | 27.1% |
| Oxygen | 0.77% |
| Carbon (bass) | 0.30% |
| Iron | 0.16% |
| Neon | 0.12% |
| Nitrogen | 0.09% |
| Silicon | 0.07% |
| Magnesium | 0.05% |
| Sulphur | 0.04% |

## 2.3 SOLAR RADIATION

The Sun emits electromagnetic waves that carry energy. Solar radiation is the energy emitted by the sun in all directions through space in the form of electromagnetic waves. There is no life on Earth without solar radiation. It is directly or indirectly responsible for phenomena such as plant photosynthesis, maintaining a planet temperature suitable for life, and wind formation. Solar radiation is measured on the horizontal surface with instruments such as pyranometers, pyrheliometers, sunshine recorders, solarimeters, etc. Watt per square metre (W/$m^2$) is the unit of measurement.

- **Solar Insolation:**The amount of solar energy received by the earth's surface at a specific geographic location. It is usually measured in kilowatt-hour per square meter (kWh/$m^2$).
- **Solar Irradiance:** This is the amount of solar energy incident on a surface per unit area per unit time. It is represented in kWh/$m^2$/sec or kWh/$m^2$/day.

### 2.3.1 Types of Solar Radiation

The solar radiation spectrum can be classified as:

Depending on the wavelength or type of light:

- **Ultraviolet (UV) rays:**It covers the wavelength range of 100-380 nm on the solar spectrum. It is invisible to the human eyes and has the most serious effect on the skin in the form of sunburns. It is divided into three bands: Ultraviolet C (UVC) in the range of 100-280 nm, Ultraviolet B (UVB) in the range of 280-315 nm and Ultraviolet A (UVA) in the range of 315-380 nm.

- **Visible light:** The visible light covers the wavelength range of 380-750 nm. The longest visible wavelength is of red colour (650-750 nm) and shortest is of violet colour (380-450).

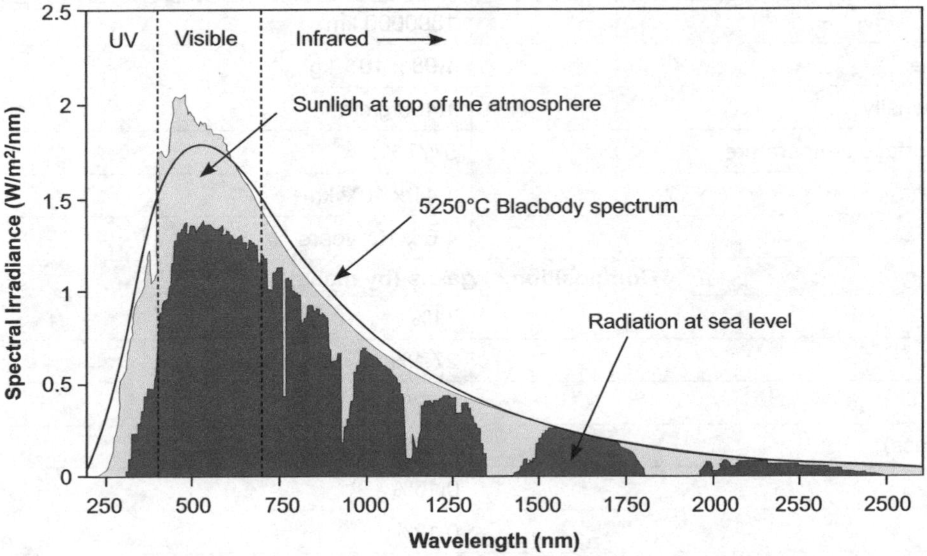


**Fig. 2.1:** Solar radiation spectrum
(**Source:** Wikimedia Commons)

- **Infrared (IR) Region:** Its wavelength range is from 750 nm to 1 mm. It accounts for a significant portion of the solar radiation that reaches the earth's surface. It is further subdivided into three parts: Infrared A (750 nm -1400 nm), Infrared B (1400 nm – 3000 nm) and Infrared C (3000 nm -1 mm).

Depending on how the solar radiation strikes the earth's surface:

- **Direct/Beam radiation:**It is the portion of solar radiation that does not get absorbed or scattered in the atmosphere and instead reaches directly. If it is interrupted by an opaque object, it casts a shadow.
- **Diffuse radiation:** This is the solar radiation which reaches the earth surface after multiple detours due to scattering by molecules and particulates present in the atmosphere.
- **Global/Total radiation:**It is sum of direct and diffuse radiation that falls on any horizontal surface on the earth.

**Global radiation = Beam radiation + Diffuse radiation**

## 2.4 SOLAR MAP OF INDIA: AVAILABILITY OF SOLAR RADIATION

Because of the abundance of solar radiation in almost every part of the country, India has a high potential for solar power generation. India has approximately 300 days of direct sunlight per year. During the summer, approximately 90% of India receives significant amounts of solar radiation. The daily long-term average of global horizontal irradiance (GHI) received ranges from 3 to 6.6 kWh/m$^2$. In different parts of the country, the average annual total of GHI ranges from 1095 to 2392 kWh/m$^2$. Table 2.2 shows the availability of average daily solar irradiance by state.

**Table 2.2:** State wise average daily solar irradiance

| State | Solar Irradiance Level (kWh/m$^2$/day) |
|---|---|
| Rajasthan | 5-7 |
| Gujrat | 4-4.7 |
| Odisha | 4-4.7 |
| Karnataka | 3.5-4.0 |
| Haryana | 3.5-4.5 |
| Andhra Pradesh | 3-4.5 |
| Maharashtra | 3-4 |
| Himanchal Pradesh | 3-4 |
| Jammu Kashmir | 3-4 |
| Madhya Pradesh | 2.9-4 |
| Uttar Pradesh | 2.9-3.9 |

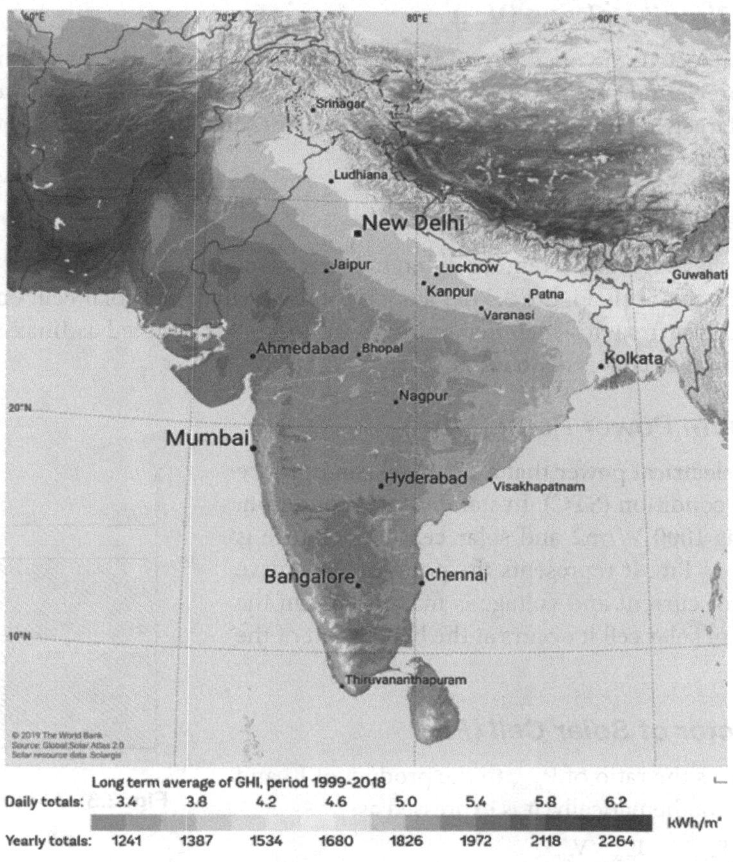


**Fig. 2.2:** Solar radiation map of India
(**Source:** Global Solar Atlas 2.0, Solar resource data: Solargis)

## 2.5 SOLAR PHOTOVOLTAIC (PV)

Solar photovoltaic is the process of directly converting sunlight into electricity using a device known as a solar cell or photovoltaic cell. Solar cells are made of semiconductor materials. Different types of semiconductor materials are used to manufacture various types of solar cells. Silicon (Si) is the most commonly used semiconductor material in the fabrication of solar cells. At the moment, silicon semiconductor is used to manufacture approximately 90 per cent of the PV modules on the market. Daryl Chaplin, Gerald Pearson, and Calvin Souther Fuller created the first practical solar cell in 1954 at Bell laboratories in the United States. Initially, it was used to supply electrical power to satellites orbiting the Earth.

### 2.5.1 Solar Cell Parameters

#### *2.5.1.1 Short Circuit Current ($I_{sc}$)*

When the voltage across the cell terminals is zero, current flows through the solar cell. The solar cell is short-circuited in this condition. The maximum current produced by a solar cell is denoted as Isc.

#### *2.5.1.2 Open Circuit Voltage ($V_{oc}$)*

When no load is connected, the open circuit voltage is measured across the two terminals of the solar cell. Voc is the abbreviation for it. This voltage is affected by the manufacturing technique and cell temperature, but is largely unaffected by the intensity of solar radiation. The typical value of open circuit voltage is 0.5 to 0.6 volts.

#### *2.5.1.3 V-I Characteristics of Solar Cell*

A graph of output voltage versus current for different levels of solar insolation and cell temperature is the V-I characteristic of a solar cell. Figure 2.3 depicts a typical V-I curve of a solar cell. Pmax represents the maximum power. The current at which maximum power occurs is denoted as Imax, and the voltage at which maximum power occurs is denoted as $V_{max}$.

#### *2.5.1.4 Maximum Power Point (MPP)*

It is the maximum electrical power that a solar cell can produce under standard test condition (STC). In standard test condition, the solar intensity is 1000 W/m2 and solar cell temperature is 25oC. It is denoted as Pm. It represents the point on V-I curve where the product of current and voltage is maximum. On the V-I curve (Fig. 2.3) of solar cell it occurs at the bend point of the curve.

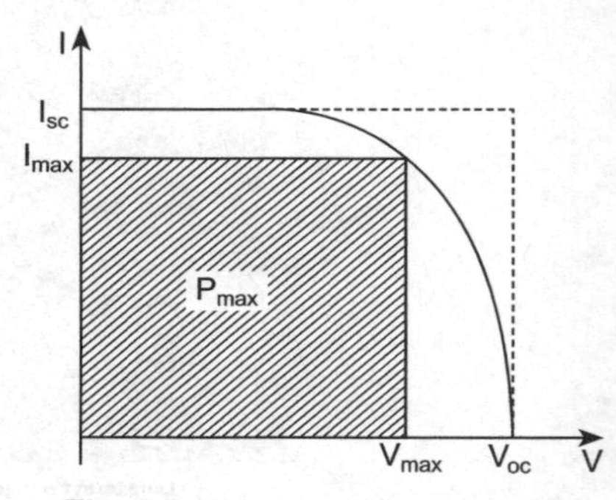


**Fig. 2.3:** V-I curve of a solar cell

#### *2.5.1.5 Fill Factor of Solar Cell (FF)*

Fill factor is defined as the ratio of $P_{max}$ to the product of $I_{sc}$ and $V_{oc}$ of the solar cell. Mathematically, it is expressed as:

$$FF = \frac{P_{max}}{I_{sc} \times V_{oc}} = \frac{I_{max} \times V_{max}}{I_{sc} \times V_{oc}} \quad (2.1)$$

### 2.5.1.6 Efficiency of Solar Cell

The efficiency of a solar cell is defined as the ratio of maximum electrical power output to the optical power incident on the solar cell. Mathematically, it is represented as:

$$\text{Efficiency} = \frac{P_{max}}{P_{in}} = \frac{I_{max} \times V_{max}}{I(t) \times A_c} = \frac{FF \times I_{sc} \times V_{oc}}{I(t) \times A_c} \quad (2.2)$$

Where, $I_{max}$ and $V_{max}$ are the current and voltage for maximum power corresponding to solar intensity I(t).

**Example 2.1:** Calculate the fill factor for a solar cell that has the following parameters:
$V_{OC} = 0.2\ V$, $I_{sc} = 5.5\ mA$, $V_{max} = 0.125\ V$, $I_{max} = 3\ mA$.

**Solution:**

From Eq. (2.1) we have,

$$\text{Fill factor (FF)} = \frac{I_{max} \times V_{max}}{I_{sc} \times V_{oc}}$$

Substituting given values of $V_{OC}$, $I_{sc}$, $V_{max}$ *and* $I_{max}$, we get

$$\text{Fill factor} = \frac{I_{max} \times V_{max}}{I_{sc} \times V_{oc}} = \frac{0.125 \times 3}{0.2 \times 5.5} = \mathbf{0.34}$$

**Example 2.2:** Calculate the efficiency of a single solar cell of dimension 10cm x 10cm which produces a voltage of 0.5 V and a current up to 2.5 A. The solar intensity is 800 W/m$^2$.

**Solution:**

Given, $I_{max}$ = 2.5 A, $V_{max}$= 0.5 V, solar intensity I(t) = 800 W/m$^2$

Area of solar cell Ac = 10 cm x 10 cm = 100 cm$^2$ =100 x 10$^{-4}$ m$^2$.

From Eq. (2.2) we have

$$\text{Cell Efficiency} = \frac{I_{max} \times V_{max}}{I(t) \times A_c} = \frac{2.5 \times 0.5}{800 \times 100 \times 10^{-4}} = 0.156$$

In percentage, efficiency = 0.156 x 100% = **15.6 %**

**Example 2.3:** If a solar intensity of 500 W/m$^2$ is incident on a solar cell of area 3 m$^2$. Calculate the power output of the cell. If the efficiency of cell is 12%.

**Solution:**

Given, Solar intensity I (t) = 500 W/m$^2$, Area of solar cell $A_c$ = 3 m$^2$,

Cell efficiency = 12% = 0.12

$$\text{We know that, Cell Efficiency} = \frac{Pout}{PinI(t) \times A_c} = \frac{Pout}{I(t) \times A_c}$$

Or, Power output, $P_{out}$= cell efficiency x I (t) x $A_c$= (0.12 x 500 x 3) Watt = **180 Watt**

## 2.5.2 Working of Photovoltaic (Solar) Cell: Photovoltaic Effect

When a photovoltaic cell is exposed to sunlight, it produces voltage or current. It is called as photovoltaic effect. A solar cell is essentially a p-n junction diode. A typical silicon solar cell consists of a boron-doped p-type semiconductor and a phosphorous-doped n-type semiconductor. When these two are connected, an electric field is created at the P-N junction. The Schematic diagram of typical solar cell is presented in Fig. 2.4.

When sunlight strikes a solar cell, photons are absorbed. Some photons have energies greater than the energy difference between the valance and conduction bands of the solar cell's semiconductor material. After absorbing such a photon, an electron in the semiconductor material jumps to the conduction band, forming an electron-hole pair. These are known as light-generated electrons and holes. The electric field created at the p-n junction gives these electrons and holes momentum and direction. The electron near the p-n junction moves to the n-type side, while the hole near the junction moves to the p-type side. As a result, a potential difference is created between the two sides of the junction, and if the two sides are connected by an external load, current flows from positive to negative.

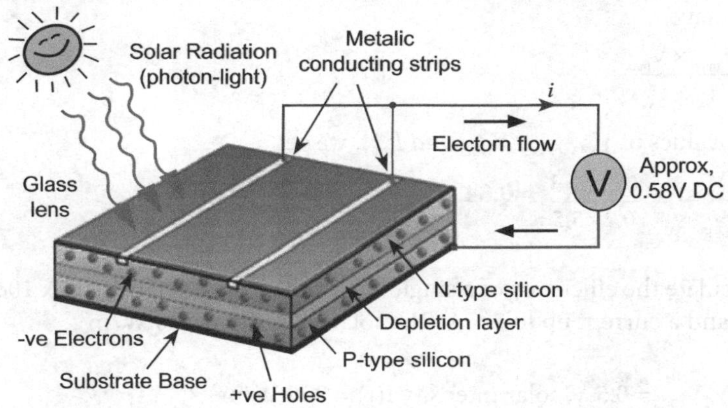


**Fig. 2.4:** Working of a solar cell

A typical single photovoltaic cell is about the size of a compact disc (CD). Due to its small size, a single solar cell can only generate a limited voltage and current. It can generate 0.5-0.6 volts of direct current voltage. The power generated by a solar cell is determined by its efficiency and size.

## 2.5.3 Types of Photovoltaic Cells

Photovoltaic cells are divided into two broad categories, crystalline solar cells and thin film solar cells.

### *2.5.3.1 Crystalline Solar Cells: First Generation*

At the moment, the majority of solar cells on the market (about 90%) are made from crystalline silicon (c-Si) wafers. These cells are cut from large silicon ingots. Ingots are solid metal pieces that are typically prepared in the shape of bricks. Silicon ingots are grown in laboratories using crystal growth processes such as the Czochralski (CZ) process. It could take up to a month for silicon ingot to grow. During the growing process, these ingots can take the form of a single or multiple crystals. The single crystals are used to make monocrystalline (mono-Si) solar cells. Single crystal wafers are typically 125 mm x 125 mm or larger in size, with a pseudo square shape. Monocrystalline silicon cells are typically coloured and cylindrical in shape. Multicrystalline or polycrystalline (multi-Si or Poly c-Si) solar cells are made up of multiple crystals. These are constructed from square silicon substrate cut from polycrystalline ingots grown in a quartz crucible. Multi crystalline wafers are typically 100 mm x 100 mm or larger and square shape.

The efficiencies of commercial crystalline silicon solar cells are in the range of 16-18 per cent for monocrystalline cells and 15-17% for polycrystalline cells. The manufacturing process of crystalline solar cells is presented in Fig. 2.5.

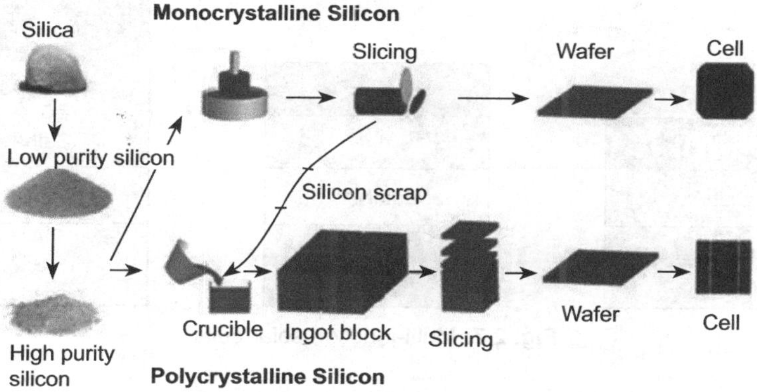


**Fig. 2.5:** Manufacturing process of crystalline silicon solar cells
(**Source:** Saga, T. Advances in crystalline silicon solar cell technology for industrial mass production. *NPG Asia Mater* 2, 96–102 (2010))

### 2.5.3.2 Thin Film Solar Cells: Second Generation

Thin film solar cells are 100 times thinner than crystalline silicon solar cells. These are made from amorphous silicon (a-Si). In contrast to crystalline silicon, atoms in amorphous silicon are randomly arranged. Thin film solar cells use less material than crystalline silicon cells, making them less expensive. However, efficiency remains low at 6-7%. Thin film solar cells are primarily made of compound semiconductors such as cadmium telluride (CdTe) and copper indium gallium di-selenide (CIGS). Because of their smaller size, they can be made more flexible in design as shown in Fig. 2.6 (a). As a result, they can be laminated on a building's windows and roofs, as shown in the Fig. 2.6 (b).

**Fig.2.6 (a):** Thin film solar cells

**Fig. 2.6 (b):** Thin film cell laminated on the window

### 2.5.3.3 Multijunction Solar Cells: Third Generation

By combining the best features of crystalline and thin film solar cells, third generation solar cell technology aims to improve the performance and efficiency of first and second generation silicon solar cells. These cells are made of organic polymers and amorphous silicon. They have multiple junctions made of different layers of semiconductor materials. These cells are more cost effective and efficient than crystalline and thin film solar cells. The various configurations of multijunction solar cells are show in Fig. 2.7.

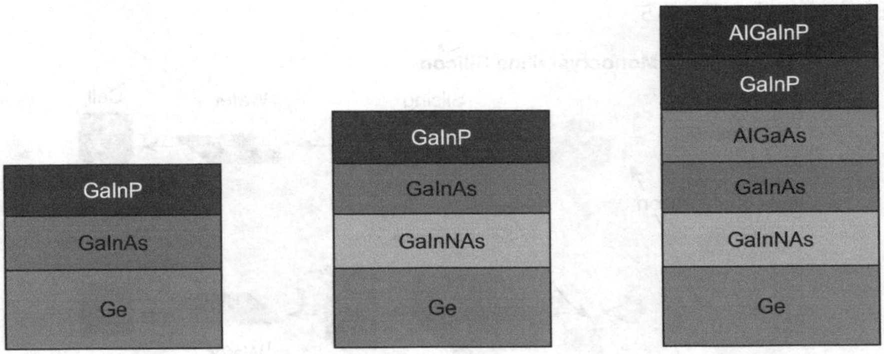


**Fig. 2.7:** Multi-junction solar cells

## 2.6 PHOTOVOLTAIC (PV) MODULE OR SOLAR PANEL

A single solar panel typically produces a very low voltage of 0.5 - 0.6 volts. This voltage is insufficient for most practical applications. A larger voltage and current can be generated by connecting a number of solar cells together. Module consisting of thirty six number of cells arranged in series connection in shown in Fig. 2.8.

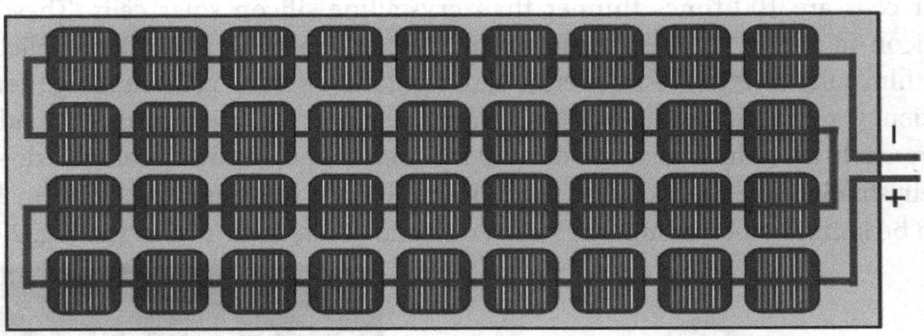


**Fig. 2.8:** PV module with 36 solar cells connected in series

PV modules or solar panels are constructed by connecting solar cells in series to produce the desired current and voltage. Photovoltaic panels are available in a variety of sizes and shapes, depending on the desired power output. A typical crystalline PV module contains very thin silicon solar cells (thickness of about 300 micron). A string of cells is placed between a top glass cover (toughened glass with high transmittivity), an encapsulate (transparent and insulating layer of EVA (ethylene vinyl acetate), and a back cover to provide strength and protect the cells from damage. The back cover is made of an insulating teldar sheet or a transparent glass sheet. An outer metallic frame is attached for strength and easy mounting on the structures. At the back of the module, a terminal box with positive and negative strings is also installed.

There are two types of crystalline PV modules available, depending on whether the back cover is opaque tedlar or transparent glass. I Glass-to-tedlar or opaque PV module with tedlar back cover and ii) Gass-to-Glass or semi-transparent PV module with glass back cover, as shown in Figs. 2.9 (a) and 2.9 (b).

The power outputof a PV module is affected by solar intensity, solar cell temperature, solar cell electrical efficiency, and load resistance. The majority of module manufacturers produce modules with 12 V or 24 V output voltage.

Fig. 2.9 (a): Opaque PV Module

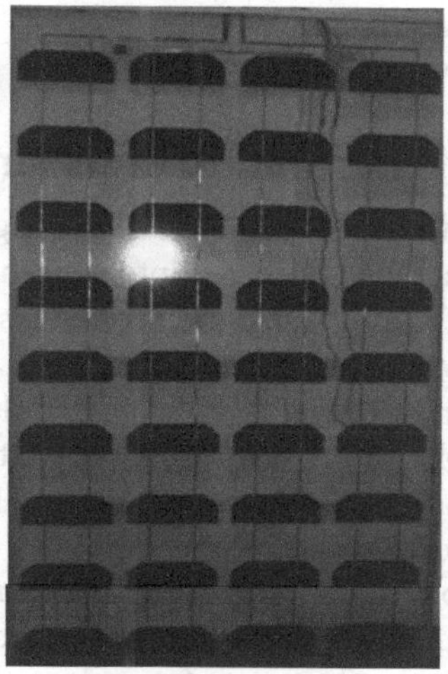

Fig. 2.9 (b): Semi-transparent PV module

## 2.7 PHOTOVOLTAIC (PV) ARRAY

Many PV modules are connected in series or parallel in larger PV plants. A photovoltaic (PV) array is a system made up of a number of PV modules that are electrically connected together in either series or parallel. Connecting many PV modules in series results in higher voltage, while connecting many PV modules in parallel results in higher current. In general, series connections are preferred to increase voltage. For example, if two PV modules are connected in series, the voltage doubles while the current remains constant. Even if the voltage, current, and power ratings are nominally the same, mixing PV modules from different manufacturers in a single PV array is not recommended. The transition from a single solar cell to a PV array is described in Fig. 2.10.

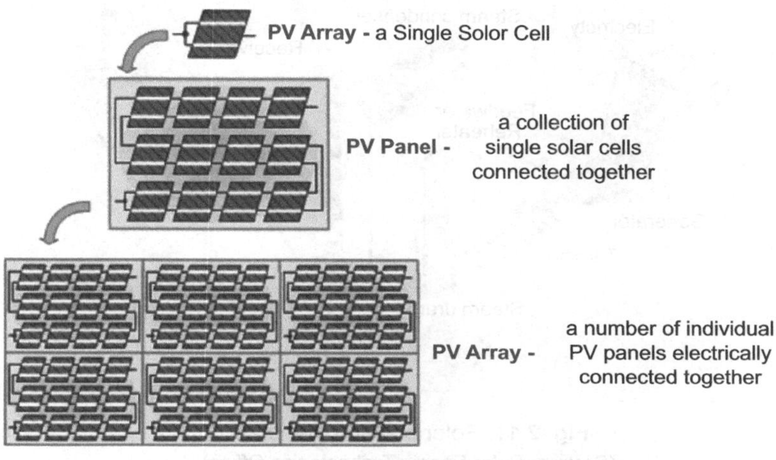


Fig. 2.10: PV cell, module and array

## 2.8 SOLAR POWER PLANTS

Solar power plants are electricity generation plants that use solar energy to generate electrical power. Solar energy can be used to generate electricity in two ways:

(i) Solar thermal power plants
(ii) Solar PV power system

### 2.8.1 Solar Thermal Power Plants

Solar thermal power plants heat a fluid to a high temperature using solar energy. This fluid conducts heat to water, which is then converted into superheated steam. The steam produced at a temperature higher than the boiling point at absolute pressure is known as superheated steam. This superheated steam is used to run powerplants' steam turbines. A mechanical generator converts the turbine's mechanical energy into electricity. Solar thermal power plants are essentially the same as traditional fossil fuel-based thermal power plants; the only difference is that sunlight is used to generate steam instead of burning fossil fuels in solar thermal power plants (coal, oil, natural gas). Solar concentrators are commonly used in these plants to concentrate the sun's rays on a single point in order to achieve high temperatures. Concentrating solar power (CSP) plants use mirrors or reflectors to concentrate solar radiation in order to power traditional steam turbines. There are various types of solar thermal power plants that use various mirrors and reflectors to focus the sun's rays on one point.

#### *2.8.1.1 Solar Power Tower*

A solar power tower is a large-scale electricity generation system. It consists of a large tower that serves as the primary receiver of solar energy. It works by directing the sun's rays to the top of the central tower via thousands of mirrors. Heliostats are a large number of flat and sun tracking mirrors. The heat transfer fluid is heated in a mounted heat exchanger after the receiver collects the sun's heat. This hot fluid is then used to generate steam for a conventional steam turbine and generator at the bottom of the tower, which generates electricity. Initially, water and steam were used as heat transfer fluids in most solar power tower plants.To maximise temperature, some advanced designs employ high temperature molten salts. Figure 2.11 depicts a schematic diagram of a typical solar power tower plant.

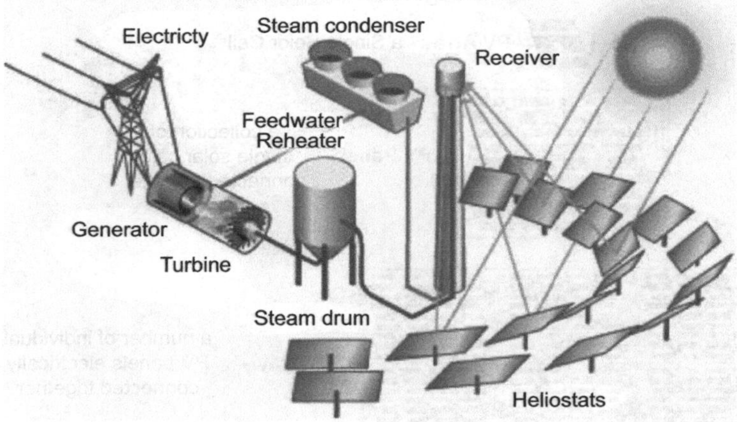


**Fig. 2.11:** Solar power tower plant
**(Source:** Solar Energy Technologies Office)

#### 2.8.1.2 Parabolic Trough Solar Power Plant

The most common type of CSP device is a parabolic trough. It is essentially a solar thermal collector that is used to concentrate the sun's rays along a specific line. It is made up of parabolic mirrors with metallic polish on the concave side. Because of its parabolic shape, it can focus solar radiation along the focal line of the trough. It is powerful enough to focus the sun's rays.

Figure 2.12 depicts a schematic diagram of a parabolic trough solar power plant. It is made up of a long metal receiver pipe filled with heat transfer fluid (HTF), usually synthetic oil. Pipe is installed along the trough's focal line. When sunlight strikes the parabolic trough collectors, it is concentrated along the receiver pipe. The receiver absorbs concentrated solar energy, and the temperature of HTF inside the receiver pipe rises to around 390 degrees Celsius. The heat is then transferred from the HTF to the working fluid (WF), which is typically water, via heat exchangers 1 (pre-heater) and 2. (boiler). Superheated steam of water is produced as a result of this heat transfer. This steam is then used to power the conventional steam turbine, which generates electricity via a generator. Exhausted steam is allowed to pass through a condenser, where it is converted into water and then pumped back to the heat exchanger via a pump. It is now the most commercially used and cost effective CSP plant.

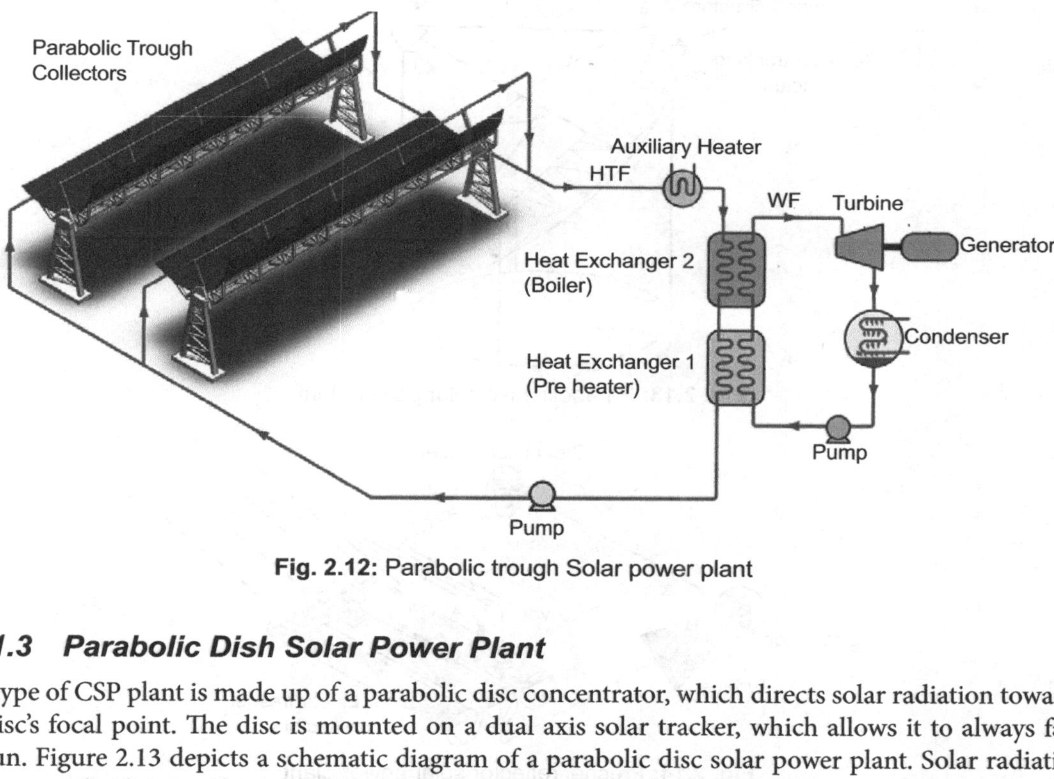


**Fig. 2.12:** Parabolic trough Solar power plant

#### 2.8.1.3 Parabolic Dish Solar Power Plant

This type of CSP plant is made up of a parabolic disc concentrator, which directs solar radiation towards the disc's focal point. The disc is mounted on a dual axis solar tracker, which allows it to always face the sun. Figure 2.13 depicts a schematic diagram of a parabolic disc solar power plant. Solar radiation incident on the disc is reflected and concentrated at the parabolic disc's focal point. At the focal point, a receiver is placed. After absorbing concentrated solar radiation, the working fluid inside the receiver is heated to a high temperature of around 750 degrees Celsius. This heated fluid is then used to power a micro-turbine or a sterling engine mounted at the receiver, which generates electricity. This type of CSP plant works as standalone system.

### 2.8.1.4 *Fresnel Reflectors Solar Power Plant*

Solar radiation heats the receiver pipe containing the working fluid in this type of power plant, which is similar to parabolic trough collectors. Fresnel reflectors are typically made up of 10 to 20 individuals, long and narrow Fresnel lenses with little or no curvature. Each reflector is attached to a tracking system that allows it to track the sun. Figure 2.14 depicts a schematic diagram of a Fresnel reflectors solar power plant. Solar radiation reflected by Fresnel reflectors and directed at a stationary receiver. After receiving this concentrated solar radiation, the fluid inside the receiver heats up. The conventional steam turbine is powered by superheated steam. A mechanical generator generates electricity. Exhausted steam is then passed through a condenser unit, which converts steam to liquid fluid. In a close cycle, this liquid is sent back to the receiver pipes. In contrast to parabolic trough power plants, these plants typically use a direct steam collection system rather than a heat transfer fluid and heat exchanger to improve efficiency and lower costs.

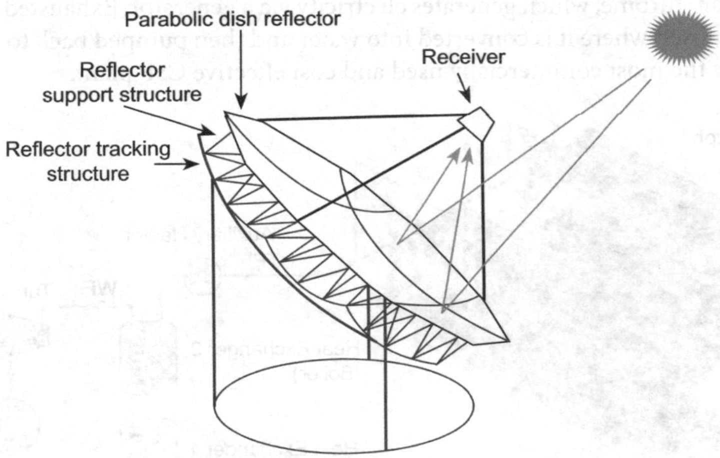


**Fig. 2.13:** Parabolic disc solar power plant

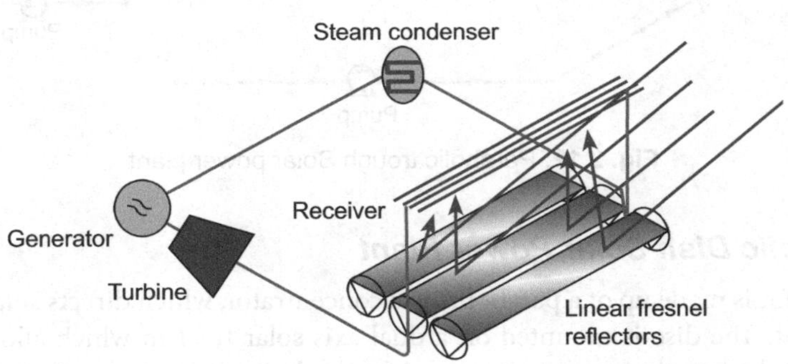


**Fig. 2.14:** Fresnel reflector solar power plant

## 2.8.2 Solar PV Power Systems

Solar PV power generation is the process converting solar energy directly into electrical power using PV modules. In the PV system, a number of PV modules are linked together to form the PV array. Although the PV array generates power when exposed to sunlight, a number of other components are required to convert, control, distribute, and store the energy generated by the PV array. The following are the primary components of the PV power generation system:

- **Solar Photovoltaic Array:** It converts sunlight directly into direct current (DC).
- **Charge Controller:** It regulates battery charging and protects it from overcharging. A battery bank is not always required in a PV system. It is only required if the PV system includes a battery bank.
- **Battery Bank:** The energy produced by the PV array that is not immediately consumed is stored in a battery bank. Few PV systems use the electricity generated immediately and do not require a battery bank.
- **Inverter:** It converts the direct current (DC) generated by the PV array to alternating current (AC) (AC). This is necessary because most of our home appliances require AC power to function.
- **Utility Meter/Power Meter:** It measures the electricity consumption by households or apartments.
- **Electric Grid:** It is an interconnected network that distributes electricity from producers to consumers. If the house is wired to the grid, any excess power generated after using and storing it in the battery will be sent to the grid.

A PV power generation plant also requires a variety of balance of system (BOS) hardware, such as wiring, overcurrent, safety and grounding equipment, surge protection and disconnect devices, and other power processing equipment. Figure 2.15 depicts the main components of a PV power generation system, as well as the relationships between them.

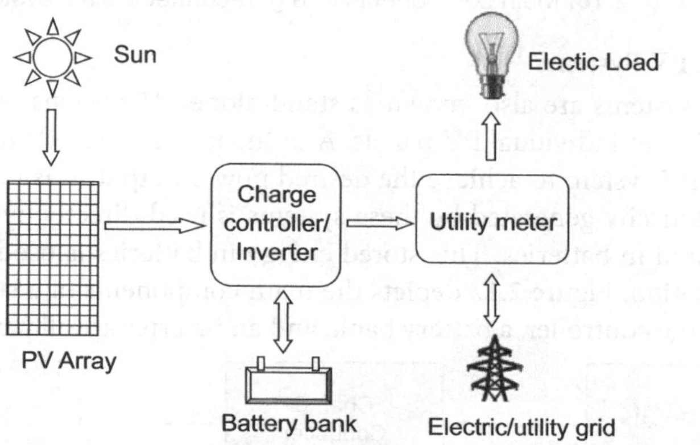


**Fig. 2.15:** Main components of a PV power generation system

### 2.8.3 Types of PV Power Systems

During the summer, it is possible that the solar PV system produces more electricity than is required by the consumer. This excess energy can be stored in batteries or fed directly into the utility grid via the PV system. PV power generation systems are classified into two types based on their functional and operational requirements, as well as how the components are connected to other power sources and the grid:

(i) Grid connected or on grid PV systems

(ii) Stand Alone or off grid PV systems

1. **Grid ConnectedPV Systems**

   Grid connected PV systems are also referred to as "on-grid," "grid-tied," or "utility-interactive." The PV array in this PV system is linked to the local power grid via a power inverter. It works in tandem with the electric utility grid. Extra power generated that is not required by users is fed into the utility grid. Figure 2.16 depicts a block diagram of the main components of a grid-connected PV system. It is made up of three major components: a PV array that converts solar energy into DC power, a grid-connected inverter that converts DC power to AC power and also generates sinusoidal power that will be used by local AC loads. The utility metre is also used to send any excess power to the power grid. To record the electricity coming from or going to the utility grid, a bi-directional metre is required.

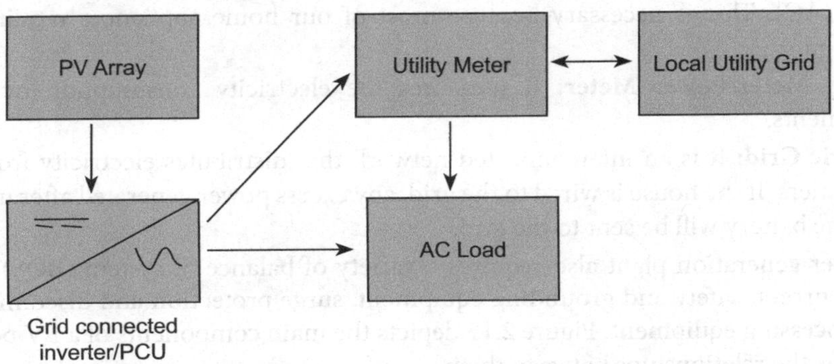


**Fig. 2.16:** Main components of a grid-connected PV system

2. **Stand Alone PV Systems**

   Off-grid PV systems are also known as stand-alone PV systems. A system like this is made up of a number of individual PV panels. A number of 12 Volt PV modules are combined in a stand-alone PV system to achieve the desired power output. It is not connected to the power grid. The electricity generated by these systems is used directly by the users, and any excess energy is stored in batteries. This stored energy in batteries is used at night or when there is no solar radiation. Figure 2.17 depicts the main components of a stand-alone PV system. PV panels, a charge controller, a battery bank, and an inverter are all part of it.

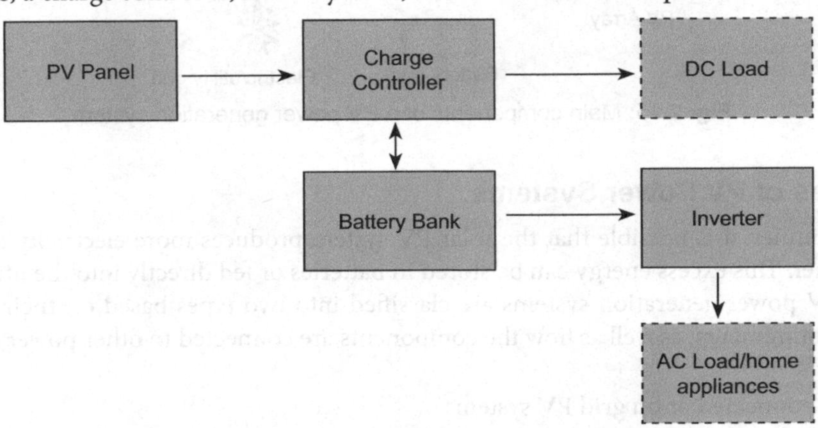


**Fig. 2.17:** Block diagram of a stand-alone PV system

Stand alone PV systems are commonly used in rural areas where access to the local electric grid is limited. The incident sunlight on the PV panel is first converted into DC power. This power can be used directly to power the DC load or stored in a battery bank via a charge controller. A charge controller is used to prevent the battery from being overcharged. An inverter converts the DC power stored in the battery to AC power, which is then sent to AC appliances.

## 2.8.4 Rooftop Solar PV Power System

PV arrays are installed on the rooftops of residential or commercial buildings in rooftop solar PV systems. It is typically installed on a building's roof where sunlight is easily and abundantly available. Figure 2.18 depicts a schematic diagram of a typical rooftop PV system. The sunlight that falls on the rooftop PV array is converted into direct current power. It is stored in a battery bank with the help of a charge controller for use when there is no grid power available. A DC-AC inverter is used to convert DC power stored in batteries into AC power to power home appliances such as light bulbs, televisions, and refrigerators. A charger is also connected between the mains and the battery to charge it using grid electricity. Figure 2.19 depicts a typical roof-mounted solar PV power system.

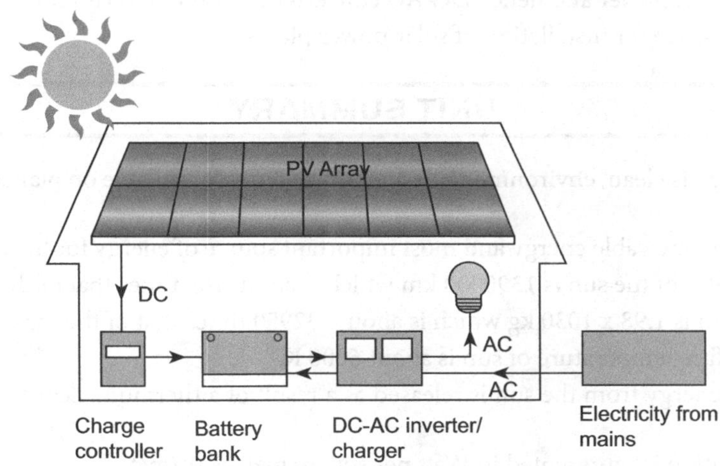


**Fig. 2.18:** Block diagram of a roof top PV system

**Fig. 2.19:** Photograph of a roof top solar PV power system

## 2.9 ADVANTAGES AND DISADVANTAGES OF SOLAR POWER PLANTS

There are several advantages and disadvantages to using solar energy:

**Advantages**

1. Solar energy is a renewable and environmentally friendly source of energy
2. It causes no pollution
3. Once solar panels are installed, energy can be produced free of cost
4. Very little operational and maintenance cost is required
5. Reduces the use of fossil fuels such as coal, oil and gas

**Disadvantages**

1. Because there is no solar power available at night, a large battery backup is required
2. High initial cost of materials and installation
3. Lower energy production in winter and on cloudy days
4. Generates DC power and hence DC-AC converter is required to run home appliances
5. Uses large space for installation of solar power plants

## UNIT SUMMARY

- Solar energy is clean, environmentally friendly and freely available on planet earth in indefinite amount.
- It is a form renewable energy and most important source of energy for life on the planet Earth.
- The diameter of the sun is 1390000 km which is about 109 times that of the diameter of earth.
- Mass of Sun is 1.98 x 1030 kg which is about 332950 times that of the mass of earth.
- Outer surface temperature of sun is about 6000 K.
- The great energy from the sun is released as a result of a thermonuclear fusion reaction in the core.
- Solar radiation is represented in Watt per square meter ($W/m^2$).
- The amount of solar energy incident on a surface per unit area per unit time is known as "solar irradiance".
- India generally have about 300 direct sunshine days per year.
- The daily received long term average of global horizontal irradiance (GHI) varies from 3 to 6.6 $kWh/m^2$.
- The average annual total of GHI in different part of the country ranges from 1095 to 2392 $kWh/m^2$.
- In India Rajasthan has the highest solar irradiance level of 5-7 $kWh/m^2/day$ followed by Gujrat and Odisha.
- Solar photovoltaic is the process in which sunlight is directly converted in to electricity by using Solar cell.
- At present about 90% of the PV modules available in the market are manufactured by using silicon semiconductor.

- The photovoltaic effect is the process to generate voltage or current in photovoltaic cell when it is exposed to sunlight.
- Solar cell is basically of a p-n junction diode.
- The size of a typical single photovoltaic cell is about the size of a compact disc (CD).
- A single solar cell can generate about 0.5-0.6 volts DC voltage.
- Photovoltaic (PV) modules or solar panels are made by connecting numbers of solar cells together in series to get desired output.
- Solar power plants are the electricity generation plants that utilizes solar energy to produce electrical power.
- Concentrating solar power (CSP) plats use mirrors or reflectors to concentrate the solar radiation to run traditional steam turbine to generate electricity.
- Solar power tower is the system used to produce electricity on a large scale.
- Parabolic trough is a solar thermal collector which is used to concentrate sun's ray along a particular focal line of the parabola.
- Now a days, parabolic trough based plants are the most commercially used and cost effective CSP plant.
- In parabolic disc solar power plants, the solar radiation is concentrated towards the focal point of the disc.
- Fresnel reflector plants are somewhat similar to the parabolic trough collectors, where solar radiation heats the receiver pipe containing the working fluid.
- Solar PV power generation is the process in which solar energy is directly converted into electrical power with the help of PV modules.

## EXERCISES

### Multiple Choice Questions

1. Solar radiation includes
   (c) Ultraviolet rays
   (b) Infrared rays
   (d) Visible light
   (d) All of these
2. A single solar cell voltage is about
   (b) 0.5 V (b) 1.0 V
   (c) 1.5 V (d) 2.0 V
3. Which converts solar energy directly into electricity
   (a) Dry cell (b) Photovoltaic cell
   (c) Battery (d) Fuel cell
4. ............... radiation is is called diffuse radiation
   (a) Infrared (b) Beam
   (c) Scattered (d) Direct

5. Solar energy is radiated from the sun in the form of
   (a) Radiowaves (b) Electromagnetic waves
   (c) Infrared waves (d) None of these
6. Common material use for making solar cells is
   (a) Copper (b) Silver
   (c) Silicon (d) Gold
7. Solar cell has
   (a) One generation (b) Two generations
   (c) Three generations (d) Four generations
8. S. I Unit of solar intensity is
   (a) $W/m^2$ (b) $W^2/m^2$
   (b) $W.m^2$ (d) $W^2.m^2$
9. Conversion efficicncy of silicon solar cells ranges from
   (a) 10 – 15% (b) 30 – 35%
   (c) 80 – 85% (d) 90 – 95%
10. Solar power generation can be done by
   (a) Parabolic trough system (b) Solar tower power
   (b) Parabolic Disc system (d) All of these
11. Whish state of India has the highest solar irradiance level
   (a) Uttar Pradesh (b) Rajasthan
   (c) Madhya Pradesh (d) Bihar
12. Commonly used photovoltaic cells are
   (a) Polymer cells (b) Organic cells
   (c) Plastic cell (d) Crystalline silicon
13. Full form of STC is
   (a) Standard test cell
   (b) Standard time cell
   (c) Solar thermal cell
   (d) Standard test condition
14. STC for photovoltaic panel is
   (a) Solar intensity is 1200 $W/m^2$and solar cell temperature is 25°C
   (b) Solar intensity is 1200 $W/m^2$and solar cell temperature is 35°C
   (c) Solar intensity is 1000 $W/m^2$and solar cell temperature is 25°C
   (d) Solar intensity is 1000 $W/m^2$and solar cell temperature is 35°C
15. PV array is
   (a) Only series combination of PV modules
   (b) Only parallel combination of PV modules
   (c) Series and parrel combination of PV modules
   (d) None of these

| Answers of Multiple Choice Questions | | | | | | | |
|---|---|---|---|---|---|---|---|
| 1. (d) | 2. (a) | 3. (b) | 4. (c) | 5. (b) | 6. (c) | 7. (c) | 8. (a) |
| 9. (a) | 10. (d) | 11. (b) | 12. (d) | 13. (d) | 14. (c) | 15. (c) | |

## Short and Long Answer Type Questions

### *Category I*

1. Define solar irradiance. In which unit it is expressed?
2. Name the instruments used to measure the solar intensity on a horizontal surface.
3. Define short circuit current, open circuit voltage and fill factor of a solar cell.
4. Draw V-I characteristic of a solar cell.
5. What is fill factor (FF) and how it is calculated.
6. What are different types of concentrators used in concentrating technology?
7. Define PV cell, PV module and PV array.

### *Category II*

1. Explain different types of solar cells based on their generation.
2. How a solar cell works. Explain with suitable diagram
3. Briefly explain different types of solar photovoltaic system using block diagram.
4. Explain the working of parabolic trough solar power plant with the help of a neat diagram.
5. What are advantages and disadvantages of solar power generation plants?

## Numerical Problems

1. Calculate the efficiency of a solar cell of area144 $cm^2$ which produces a voltage of0.6 V and a current up to 2 A. The solar intensity is 1000 $W/m^2$.

**[*Ans: 8.3%*]**

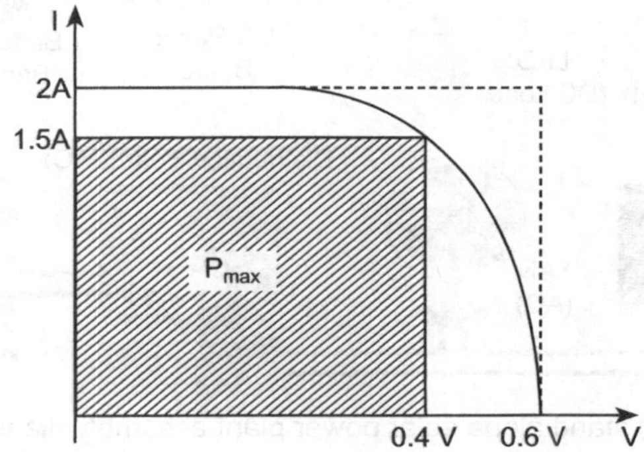


2. The V- I curve of a typical solar cell is drawn in figure. Calculate the fill factor ofthe cell.

**[ *Ans: 0.5*]**

3. A single solar cell is illuminated by a solar intensity of 800 W/m$^2$. It produces a voltage of 0.5 V and current up to 2.0 Amp. Calculate area of the cell if its electrical efficiency is 12.5%.

[*Ans: 0.10m$^2$*]

4. A rectangular PV module of dimension (1.5 m x 2.0 m) receives solar intensity of 550 W/m$^2$. If the cell efficiency is 12%, calculate the power output of the module.

[*Ans: 198 Watt*]

## PRACTICAL

## Assemble the solar PV plant to produce electric power

**Aim**

To install a standalone solar PV system for electricity generation

**Equipment**

PV Panels, charge controller, power inverter, DC panel board distribution panel, battery bank, connecting wires, home appliances

**Theory**

A typical stand alone solar power plant assembly diagram is shown in Fig. (i). First, you need to determine the size of solar system required. It can be determined adding up the wattages of all the electrical appliances to be used.

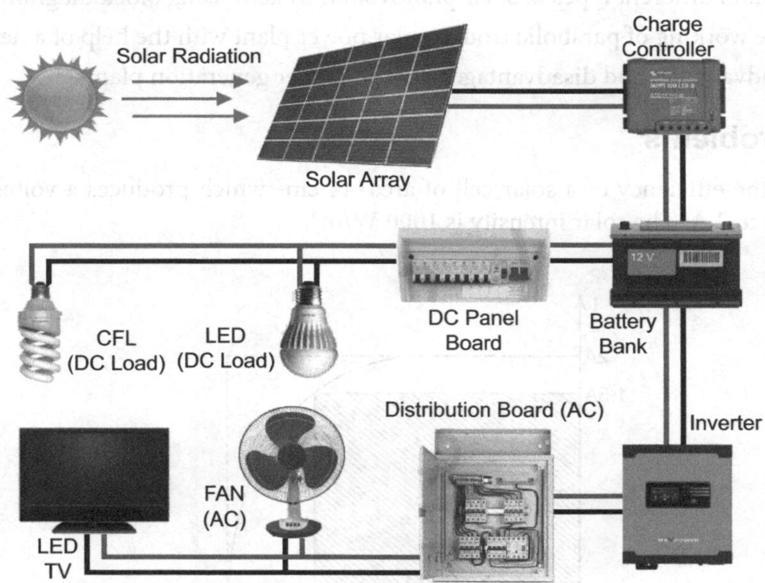


**Fig.** (i) stand alone solar power plant assembly diagram

**Procedure**

(1) Determine the energy demand by adding the wattages of all electrical appliances and the number of hours they are in use.

(2) Mount the solar panel to the mounting structure
(3) Attach the charge controller between solar panel and battery bank.
(4) Connect the battery to a DC panel board in order to power any DC appliances.
(5) Connect the battery to an inverter that converts DC power to AC power
(6) Use a distribution board to connect the inverter to AC home appliances (AC).

**Precautions**

(1) Tight connections are required. Loose wiring can reduce the efficiency of aPV panel
(2) There is a risk of short circuiting during inclement weather. As a result, high-quality connecting wires must be used.

## KNOW MORE

**Semiconductors:**
Materials can be broadly classified as conductors (e.g., metals), semiconductors, and insulators based on their current flowing capacity (e.g. ceramics). The conductor always conducts electrical current, whereas the insulator does not. Semiconductors are materials that have conductivity between conductors and insulators. Silicon (Si), Germanium (Ge), Gallium arsenide (GaAs), and other elements are examples.

**Types of semiconductors:**
Semiconductors can be classified as:

(1) Intrinsic semiconductor
(2) Extrinsic semiconductor

**Intrinsic semiconductor:**Intrinsic semiconductors are pure silicon (Si) and germanium (Ge) (Ge). It contains only one type of element. The most common intrinsic semiconductors are Si and Ge. These semiconductors have very low conductivity at room temperature.

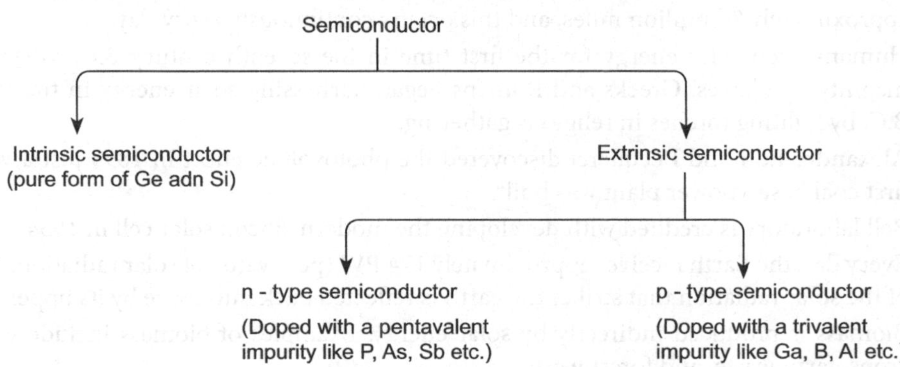


**Extrinsic semiconductor:** The conductivity of intrinsic semiconductors can be improved by adding a small amount of suitable elemental impurities. Doping is the process of introducing impurities into a pure semiconductor. Extrinsic semiconductor is a semiconductor that has been doped with impurity. Extrinsic semiconductors are further subdivided into:

(1) n-type semiconductor
(2) p-type semiconductor

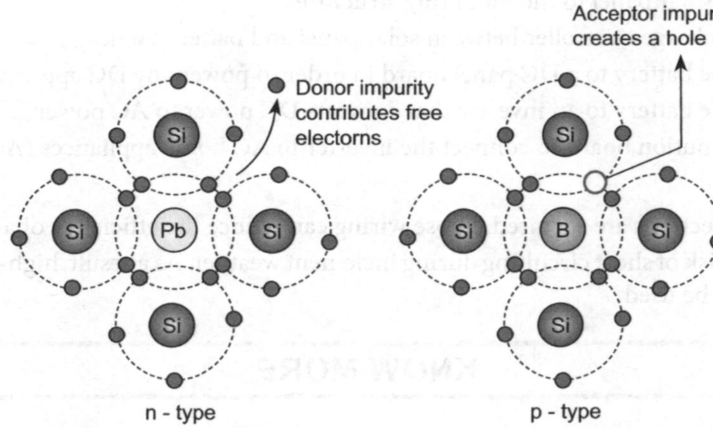


**n-type semiconductor:** When a tetravalent atom, such as Ge or Si, is doped with a pentavalent impurity, such as Pb. As shown in the figure, Pb's four electrons form a bond with four neighbouring Si atoms. The fifth electron of Pb is still free to move in the semiconductor. This type of semiconductor is known as an n-type semiconductor. These contain donor impurities, which contribute free electrons.

**p-type semiconductor:** When a tetravalent atom like Ge or Si is doped with a trivalent impurity like Boron (B). Three electrons of B form bond with three neighbouring atoms of Si. The fourth atom of Si is free and a hole or vacancy is generated in the trivalent atom B. This type of semiconductor is known as p-type semiconductor. The acceptor impurity creates a hole in this type of semiconductor.

**Interesting Facts**

- The earth receives more energy from the sun in a single hour than all humanities living on the planet require in an entire year.
- Light from the sun takes less than 10 minutes to reach the earth's surface after travelling approximately 90 million miles, and this occurs continuously every day.
- Humans used solar energy for the first time in the seventh century B.C. to start fires with magnifying glasses. Greeks and Romans began harnessing solar energy in the third century B.C. by lighting torches in religious gathering.
- Alexandre Edmond Becquerel discovered the photovoltaic effect in 1893 just a year after the first coal based power plant was built.
- Bell laboratory is credited with developing the modern silicon solar cell in 1954.
- Every day, the Earth receives approximately 174 PW (petawatts) of solar radiation. Around 30% of the solar radiation that strikes the earth is reflected back into space by its upper atmosphere.
- Biomass is produced indirectly by solar energy. Examples of biomass include wood, energy crops, farm waste, and forest waste.
- Using a solar distillation system, solar energy can assist in the production of distilled water from saline water.
- The 1970 oil crisis sparked indirect research in the field of solar energy technology.
- In the early 1950s, the space industry adopted solar technology to power spacecraft. The Vanguard 1 was the first satellite to use solar-cell-generated power.

## REFERENCES AND SUGGESTED READINGS

1. J. W. Twidella and A. Weir, *Renewable Energy Sources*, EFN Spon Ltd., UK, 2006.
2. G. N. Tiwari and R. K. Mishra, *Advanced Renewable Energy Resources*, RSC Publishing, UK, 2012.
3. C. S. Solanki, *Solar Photovoltaic Technology and Systems: A Manual for Technicians, Trainers and Engineers*, PHI Learning Pvt. Ltd., 2013.
4. N. H. Ravindranath, U. K. Rao, B. Natarajan, P. Monga, *Renewable Energy and Environment-A Policy Analysis for India*, Tata McGraw Hill.
5. R. A. Ristinen and J. J. Kraushaar, *Energy and The Environment, Second Edition*, John Willey & Sons, New York, 2006.
6. D. P. Kothari, *Renewable Energy Sources and Emerging Technologies*, PHI Learning, New Delhi, ISBN: -978-81-203-4470-9

Dynamic QR Code for Further Reading

# 3 Large Wind Power Plants

## UNIT SPECIFICS

Following major points have been discussed in the unit:

- Wind power density in various locations of India
- Various principle involved in the wind energy conversion
- Geared and direct drive type wind power plants
- Layout and working of different types of constant and variable speed electric generators
- Advantages and disadvantages of various types of large wind power plants

The wind map of India based on the wind power density at various locations has been introduced in this unit. Basic aerodynamic principles and theories like lift and drag principle, long path theory have been discussed. Electric generator is the basic unit to harness electricity from the wind energy. In this unit we shall discuss different types of generators used in large wind power plants. Different types of large wind power plants have been discussed with the help of component wise block diagram.

Together with the large and short answer type problems multiple-choice questions have beengiven for the better understanding of the reader. A list of references and suggested readings are given in the unit so that one can go through them for practice. It is important to note that for getting more information on various topics of interest some QR codes have been provided which can be scanned for relevant supportive knowledge.

There is a "Know More" section in the last of the unit. This section has been carefully designed so that the supplementary information provided in this part becomes beneficial for the reader

## RATIONALE

Wind energy is one of the important sources of renewable energy. It reduces the use of fossil fuels and hence supports the reduction of harmful greenhouse gases. India has great potential to harness wind energy. Wind energy is used to produce electrical power through wind power plants. Wind turbine and generators are the two basic parts in any wind power plant. Depending on the generation capacity of these plants, various designs of wind power plants are available worldwide. In this chapter we will be discussing the wind power plants of large generation capacity.

## PRE-REQUISITES

Basic knowledge of wind

## UNIT OUTCOMES

List of outcomes of this unit is as follows:

**U3-O1:** To know about the wind power density in various parts of India.

**U3-O2:** To understand aboutprinciples of wind energy conversion system.

**U3-O3:** To study about various types of large wind power plants.

**U3-O4:** To study about constant speed electric generators

**U3-O5:** To study about variable speed electric generators

| Unit-3 Outcomes | EXPECTED MAPPING WITH COURSE OUTCOMES (1-Weak Correlation; 2-Medium Correlation; 3-Strong Correlation) | | | | |
|---|---|---|---|---|---|
| | CO-1 | CO-2 | CO-3 | CO-4 | CO-5 |
| U3-O1 | - | 3 | - | - | - |
| U3-O2 | - | 3 | - | - | - |
| U3-O3 | - | 3 | - | - | - |
| U3-O4 | - | 3 | - | - | - |
| U3-O5 | - | 3 | - | - | - |

## 3.1 OVERVIEW

When solar radiation strikes the ground, the earth's surface temperature rises. But this rise in temperature is not uniform everywhere because the earth's surface is made up of land and water forms of different types. This uneven heating causes different air pressure from one area to another. This allows air to move from one direction to another. This **moving air is called as "wind".**

Wind is a powerful force which are being utilized by mankind since long time through various technologies like wind mills, wind turbine, wind farms or wind power plants.

**Wind Mill:**

Wind mill is a structure which is used to covert wind energy into rotational (mechanical) energy by means of some blades. These blades are called as vanes or sail. Wind mills are used for sailing ships, grinding grains and pumping ground water etc. The photograph of a wind mill installed at Kinderdijk, Netherlands is shown in Fig. 3.1.

**Fig. 3.1:** Windmills at village Kinderdijk, Netherlands.

**Wind Turbine:**

Wind turbines are used to convert the kinetic energy of wind into electrical energy. The conversion of wind energy into electrical energy is one of the successful and important renewableenergy technologies. The amount of power produced by a wind turbine depends on the size of the turbine and length of the blades in the turbine. Harnessing the electrical energy from wind is getting momentum because of the depletion and bad environmental effect of using fossil fuels. Wind energy is considered as one of the important renewable sources of energy which provides clean and green power. In 19th century wind power greatly contributed toward the economic development of many countries like Netherland, Denmark and USA.

The size of the wind turbine and the length of its blades determine how much electricity it can generate. Due to the depletion of fossil fuels and their negative effects on the environment, wind energy harvesting is becoming more popular. One of the most significant renewable energy sources that produce pure, green energy is wind energy. Wind energy had a significant impact on the economic growth of numerous nations in the 19th century, including the Netherlands, Denmark, and the United States. Live pictures of horizontal and vertical axis wind turbines are presented in Fig. 3.2 (a) and 3.2 (b).

**Fig. 3.2 (a):** Horizontal axis wind Turbine

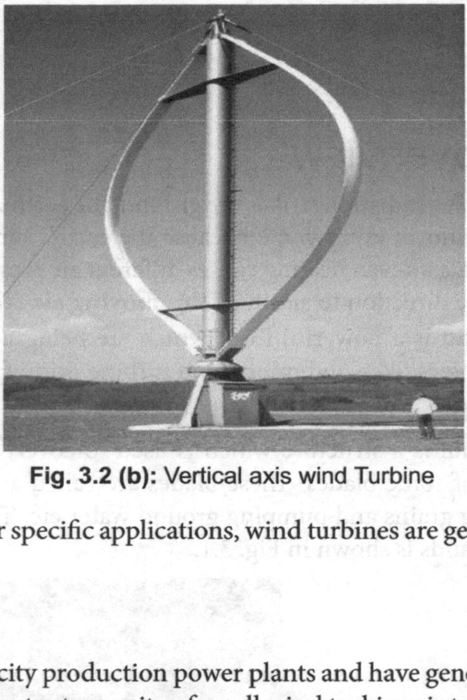

**Fig. 3.2 (b):** Vertical axis wind Turbine

Based on the power generation capacities and their specific applications, wind turbines are generally classified into two broad categories

(i) Large wind turbine and

(ii) Small wind turbines.

Large wind turbines are designed for use in electricity production power plants and have generation capacity ranging from 650 kW to 1800 kW. The power output capacity of small wind turbines is typically less than 50 kW. These turbines are intended for use in small-scale industrial, domestic, and agricultural applications.

**Wind farm or wind power plant:**

Wind farm or wind power plant also called as Wind Park or wind power station is a group of wind turbines installed at the same location for electricity production. Muppandal wind farm in Kanyakumari, Tamil Nadu as shown in the Fig. 3.3 is the largest wind farm in India with installed capacity of 1500 MW.

**Fig. 3.3:** Muppandal Windfarm Kanyakumari, Tamil Nadu

Live picture of Juiquan wind power base is depicted in Fig. 3.4. It is one of the world's biggest wind farms with the installed capacity of 20 GW.

**Fig. 3.4:** Jiuquan wind power base, China

## 3.2 WIND POWER DENSITY: WIND MAP OF INDIA

An indication for calculating the amount of wind power available at a certain area is the wind power density (WPD). It is employed to evaluate how well various locations generate wind energy. It describes the amount of wind energy flowing through unit area in unit time through a surface perpendicular to the direction of wind flow. It is expressed in Watt/sq. meter(W/m$^2$). It assists in comparing and choosing the ideal locations for wind turbines. Turbines installed at locations with higher WPD typically produce more electrical energy.

The wind power map displayed in Fig. 3.5 illustrates the density of wind at a height of 50 meters for various places in India. In the map WPD, is classified as (i) 0-100 W/m$^2$, (ii) less than 200 W/m$^2$, (iii) 200-250 W/m$^2$, (iv) 250-300 W/m$^2$, (v) 300-400 W/m$^2$, and (vi) 400-500 W/m$^2$. Most of the states in India have the power density in the range of 0-100 W/m$^2$. Few of the locations in Gujarat and Tamil Nadu have some higher value of WPD in the range of 250-300 W/m$^2$.

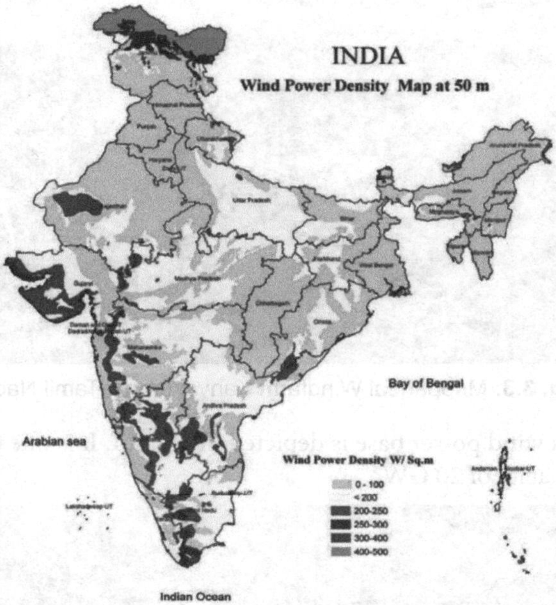


**Fig. 3.5:** Wind map of India

## 3.3 WIND TURBINE

A wind turbine is a device that transforms wind energy into electrical energy. The kinetic energy of the wind is initially transformed in wind turbines into the mechanical energy of a revolving shaft. A generator is then used to turn the mechanical energy into electrical energy. Modern wind turbines come in a variety of sizes, but practically all of them have three major sections and numerous auxiliary parts. The rotor blades, nacelle, and tower are its principal parts. Fig. 3.6 displays a schematic illustration of the various components of a typical wind turbine.

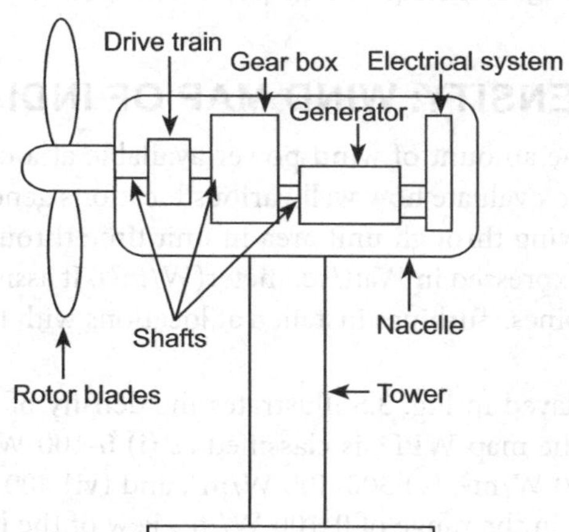


**Fig. 3.6:** Wind turbine components

- **Rotor Blades:** The blade typically has a flat side and a normally curved side. These blades are built of hollow, lightweight composite materials rather than being solid steel. Three blades are typically present. The picture of a rotor blade is presented in Fig. 3.7.
- **Nacelle:** It contains several components like drive train, shafts, gear box, generator and electrical system. The rotor blades are connected to the generator by gear box. The gear box connects the low-speed shaft to the high-speed shaft where the rotational speed is increased from about 30-60 revolution per minute (rpm) to approximately 1000-1500 rpm. The generator is then converts the rotational energy of the rotor blades to the electrical energy. A picture of gear box and generatorare shown in Figs. 3.8 (a) and 3.8 (b).

Fig. 3.7: Rotor blades in wind turbine

Fig. 3.8 (a): Gear box in wind turbine

Fig. 3.8 (b): Wind turbine generator

- **Tower:** Rotor blades and nacelle are mounted on the top of a tower. Generally, it is made with steel in round tubular shape. The height of the tower is usually 50 - 100 m and diameter is about 3 - 4 m.

## 3.4 WIND TURBINE AERODYNAMICS

Wind turbine converts the kinetic energy of wind into electrical energy. The principle of this conversion is somewhat similar to the principle behind aerodynamics of the aeroplane wings or helicopter blades.

There are two important principles by which energy is extracted from the wind, these are through the creation of either lift force or drag force (or through the combination both).

### 3.4.1 Drag and Lift Principle

When a body moves with some velocity in a fluid (air) making some angle with the direction of airflow, air exerts some force on the body. The force exerted by the air in the direction of air flow is called as the **drag force.** The force exerted in the direction normal to the airflow is called as **lift force**. If hand is put out from the window in a moving car, the hand moves towards the rear side due to the drag force and at the same time it moves in upward direction also. Hence both lift and drag forces act on a body immersed in a moving fluid. The lift and drag components are shown in Fig. 3.9.

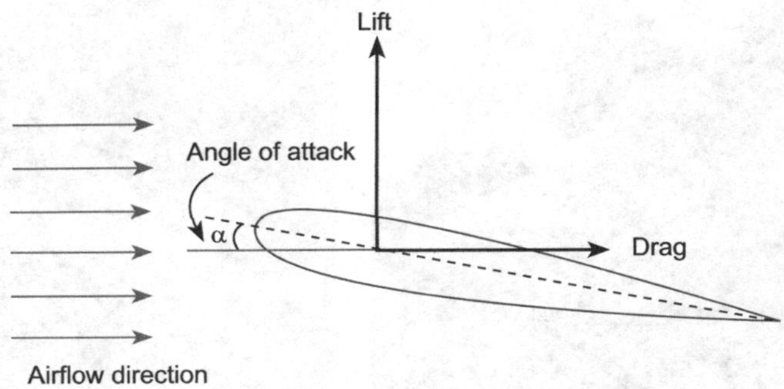


**Fig. 3.9:** Schematic diagram of lift and drag force

The lift force ($F_L$) and drag force ($D_L$) acting on a body in a fluid can be calculated as:

$$\text{Lift force } F_L = C_L \frac{1}{2} \rho . v^2 A \tag{3.1}$$

$$\text{Drag force } F_D = C_D \frac{1}{2} \rho . v^2 A \tag{3.2}$$

Where,

$C_L$ = lift coefficient
$C_D$ = drag coefficient
$\rho$ = density of the fluid (kg/m³)
v = flow velocity (m/s)
A = body area (m²)

The resultant force can be calculated as:

$$F_R = \sqrt{F_L{}^2 + F_D{}^2} \tag{3.3}$$

**Example 3.1:** Calculate the lift and drag force for an aeroplane flying with velocity 100 m/s. The wing area is 20 m², drag coefficient is 0.06 and lift coefficient is 0.7. Take the air density as 1.2 kg/m³.

**Sution:**

From Eq. (3.1) we have,

Lift force $F_L = C_L . \frac{1}{2} \rho . v^2 A .$

Given, $C_L = 0.7$; $\rho = 1.2$ kg/m³, v = 100 m/s, A = 20 m².
Substituting given values above Eq. (3.1), we get

Lift force $$F_L = \left(0.7 \text{x} \frac{1}{2} \text{x}1.2 \text{ x}100 \text{ x}100 \text{ x}20\right) \text{N}$$

$$= 84000 \text{ N} = \mathbf{84 \text{ kN}}$$

From Eq. (3.2) we have,

Drag force $$F_D = C_D.\frac{1}{2}\rho.v^2.A$$

Given, $C_D = 0.06$; $\rho = 1.2$ kg/m³, v = 100 m/s, A = 20 m².
Substituting given values above Eq. (3.2), we get

Drag force $$F_D = \left(0.06 \text{x} \frac{1}{2} \text{x}1.2 \text{ x}100 \text{ x}100 \text{ x}20\right) \text{N}$$

$$= 7200 \text{ N} = \mathbf{7.2 \text{ kN}}$$

### 3.4.2 Longer Path Theory

Longer path theory is also known as "equal transit theory". The shape of the aerofoil (rotor blade) is such that the top surface is longer than the bottom surface. Because of this, the air molecule that flows over the top surface of aerofoil travels longer distance than the air molecule which flows below the bottom surface. The theory states that the air molecules have the reach the trailing edge at the same time, and for this the molecule flowing over the top surface of the blade must travel faster than the air molecule flowing below the bottom surface. According to Bernoulli's equation the increase in velocity results a decrease in pressure. Hence at the top surface air pressure will be lower than the bottom surface. This pressure difference across the aerofoil produces the lift of t blade as shown in Fig. 3.10.

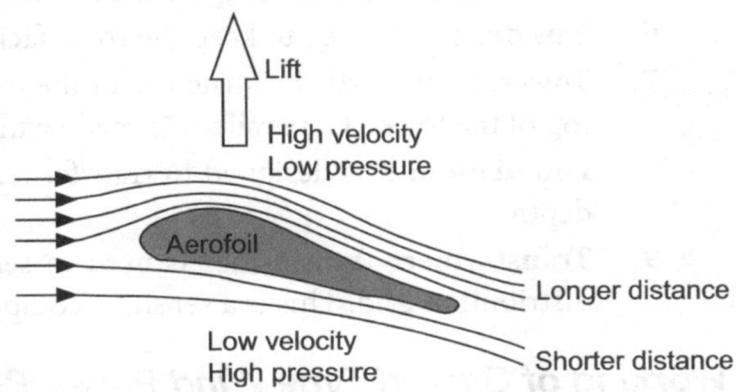


**Fig. 3.10:** Longer path theory

## 3.5 WIND POWER GENERATION: LARGE WIND POWER PLANTS

A number of wind turbines placed at the same location for the purpose of producing electricity are referred to as a wind power plant, wind energy farms or wind power station. Wind power plants vary in size from small wind power plant to large wind power plant.

Wind power plants can be classified according to their power generation capacity.

(i) **Small wind power plant:** These have the power output ranging from 10 – 50 kW. The rotor diameter is about 1-16 m.

(ii) **Medium wind power plant:**These have the power output ranging from 50-500 kW and rotor diameter of 16-50 kW.

(iii) **Large wind power plant:** These produces electricity in bulk amount for delivery to the local transmission line. The power output of these plants is ranging from 500-2000 kW and rotor diameter of 50-130 m.

Based on design and components, the two famous types of large wind power plants are

(i) Geared type

(ii) Direct drive type wind power plant.

## 3.5.1 Geared Type Wind Power Plants

These are the old and traditional wind power plants. They have complex design and require more maintenance cost. The layout of a typical geared type wind power plant is shown in Fig. 3.11.

Main components of a geared type wind power plant are:

1. **Rotor blade:** The rotor blade is designed according to the wind speed and the desired power output. The blade must be strong and light weight. Composite material like FRP (fibre reinforced plastic) is generally used for making rotor blades.
2. **Hub:** It holds the rotor blade and connects them to the shaft. It must hold the blade in its proper position to get maximum aerodynamic efficiency. It rotates in order to drive the generator.
3. **Gear box:** It is placed between rotor blade and generator. It is used to increase the rotational speed of the main shaft connected with electric generator.
4. **Generator:** It is used to convert the rotational energy of the shaft to electrical energy.
5. **Nacelle:**It consists of components shafts, gear box and generator unit.
6. **Yaw drive:** It is used to keep the rotor facing the wind direction all the time.
7. **Tower:** It supports the structure of the turbine. Rotor blades and nacelle are mounted on the top of the tower. Generally, it is made with steel in round tubular shape.
8. **Foundation:** It is designed to transfer and spread the load of the wind turbine to the soil at depth.
9. **Transformer:** Transformer is used to send the electricity produced by wind turbine to the distribution grid. This is a sensitive component of the wind turbine.

### *Working of Geared Type Wind Power Plants*

Wind blows on the rotor blade connected with the shaft. The shaft starts rotating. Rotational speed of the shaft increases up to around 1500 rpm with the help of gear box. The shaft rotating with high speed drives the generator which produces the electrical energy. With the help of a transformer the produced energy is feed to the local distribution grid for the use of consumers.

### *Advantages and Disadvantages of Geared Type Wind Power Plants*

**Advantages:**

1. Light in weight
2. Provides high torque to the shaft
3. Able to provide high speed operation and is economical to use

**Disadvantages:**

1. Very old and complicated design
2. Gears cause friction losses up to 10%.

3. Not so reliable to use.
4. Required coupling and heavy mounting structure
5. High maintenance is required because of so many moving parts.

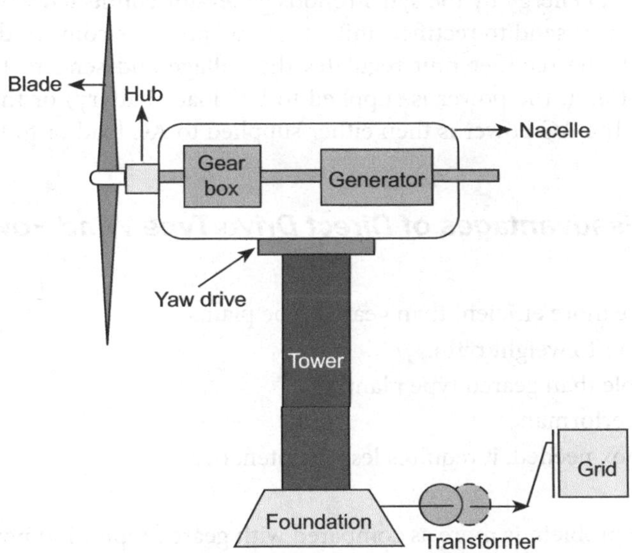


**Fig. 3.11:** Geared type wind power plant

## 3.5.2 Direct Drive Type Wind Power Plant

Gears are the most complicated part in the geared type wind power plants. Removing the gearbox from the turbine eliminates the most complex part of the turbine and it improves its performance and reliability.

In direct drive type wind power plants, the rotor is directly connected to the generator and no gear box is there in between blade and generator. The layout of a direct drive type wind power plants is shown in Fig. 3.12.

Main components of typical direct drive type power plants are:

1. **Rotor blades:** Turbine blades are made with lightweight materials for better performance.
2. **Synchronous generator:** A synchronous generator made with permanent magnet is used. It converts the mechanical power of the shaft into electrical power.
3. **Rectifier unit:** Rectifier is used to convert AC power generated by generator to the DC power for batteries.
4. **Voltage regulator:** It regulates the output voltage coming from the rectifier. It sends the regulated output voltage to D.C control unit
5. **Surplus energy dump:** It is used to divert the excess power when batteries are fully charged.
6. **D.C control unit:** It supply the controlled DC power to the DC loads.
7. **Inverter:** It converts the D.C power into A.C power. This AC power is supplied to the AC load or sent to grid system
8. **Battery:** It is connected to the D.C control unit and stores the D.C power.

### Working of Direct Drive Type Wind Power Plants

Rotor blade is rotated by the wind passes through the propeller blade. Blades are flat in shape which increases the lift and rotor shaft start rotating. The rotational (mechanical) energy of the shaft in then converted into the electrical energy by the synchronous generator connected with the shaft. The power coming from the generator is send to rectifier unit where AC power is converted to DC power. Voltage regulator connected with the rectifier unit regulates the voltage and send to DC control unit. With the help of a DC control unit, the power is supplied to DC load (battery) or through an inverter it is converted to AC power. The AC power is then either supplied to AC load or to the local electrical grid for distribution.

### Advantages and Disadvantages of Direct Drive Type Wind Power Plants

**Advantages:**

1. These plants are more efficient than geared type plants
2. It has high power to weight ratio.
3. It is more reliable than geared type plants
4. It gives better performance
5. Since no gear box needed, it requires less maintenance.

**Disadvantages:**

1. Transportation problem is more as compared with geared type wind power plant
2. Mechanical and electromagnetic structure need to be improved.

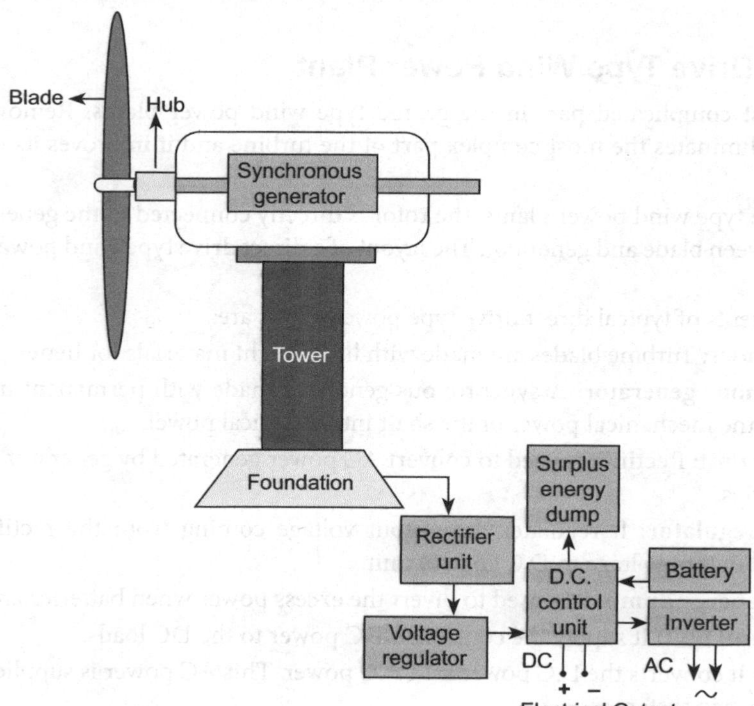


**Fig. 3.12:** Direct drive type wind power plant

## 3.6 WIND TURBINE ELECTRIC GENERATORS

Wind turbine electric generator converts the wind power into electrical power. It consists of various components like propeller blades, gear box, generator etc. Several identical units are installed in a wind farm to get desired power output. The total electrical power produced by various units is send to distribution network or to the stand alone load for further use.

Based on the type of load demand, operation and wind power rating, different types of electric generators and control methods can be selected. For small power rating DC generators can be used. For large power rating induction generator or synchronous generators are preferred. The generator is usually connected to the turbine blades through a gear. Based on the system speed, electric generators are classified as:

(i) Constant Speed Electric generators
(ii) Variable Speed Electric generators

### 3.6.1 Constant Speed Electric Generators

In constant speed wind electric generator, the turbine always rotates with a fixed generator/rotor speed during its operation and it does not depend on the wind speed. The generator torque of constant rotor speed is generally required for large generators. There are two types of constant speed electric generators based on the rotor design:

**(1) Squirrel Cage Induction Generators (SCIG):**Squirrel cage induction generator uses a rotor of squirrel cage shape. Rotor has the conducting barsplaced in the slots. The bars are permanently shorted at both ends by using copper or aluminium rings. These rings are called as **end rings.** The bars form the shape of squirrel cage as shown in Fig. 3.13 (a). It is very simple and highly efficient design. The maintenance cost is very low for these machines. Speed of the generator does not depend on the wind speed and it works very close to its rated speed. Speed variation in SCIG is very small against the variation in wind speed. The picture of a typical SCIG is shown in Fig. 3.13 (b).

**Fig. 3.13 (a):** Squirrel cage rotor

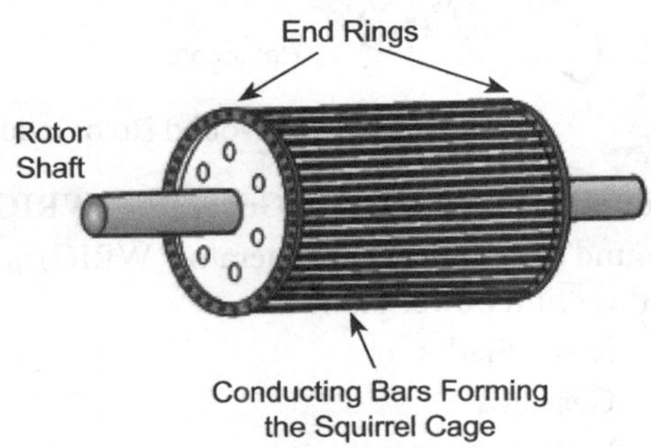


**Fig. 3.13 (b):** Squirrel cage induction generator

**Squirrel Cage Induction Generator (SCIG) connected in a wind power plant:**

Induction machines are used as motors at large scale in the power industries. Because of their simple design, low cost, low maintenance and working without external DC source, these machines are also being used as generators in wind power plants. The block diagram of a wind power plant connected with SCIG is shown in Fig. 3.14. The turbine blades are coupled to SCIG through a gear box. It works as at constant speed. The power generated by the SCIG is first converted to DC by an AC to DC converter. The DC power is then converted into AC through a DC to AC converter. The output voltage is stepped up by a 3-phase step-up transformer and sent to utility grid for distribution.

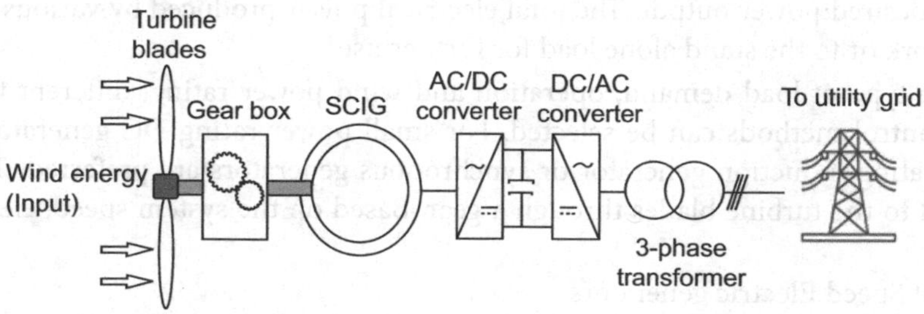


**Fig. 3.14:** Block diagram of SCIG based wind power plant

(2) **Wound Rotor Induction Generator (WRIG):** In this type of generator an external mechanism is required to control the rotor output. The windings in the rotor are connected to power electronics. They also use variable resistors along with the power electronics and brushes. These variable resistors control the rotor voltage to maintain continuous power supply. Their design is quite complicated and they are more costly than SCIG. The schematic diagram and live picture of a wound rotor induction generator is shown in Fig. 3.15.

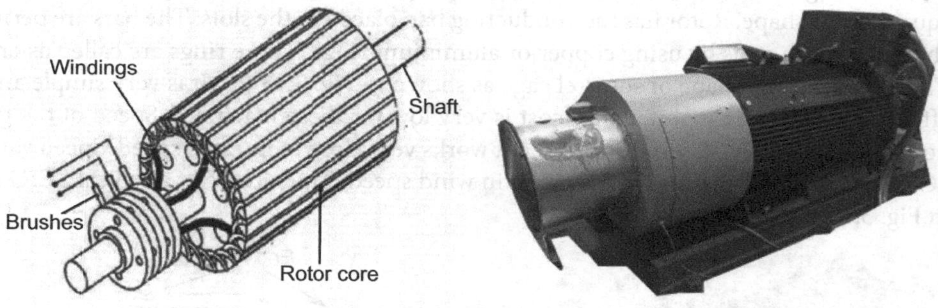


**Fig. 3.15:** Wound Rotor Induction Generator (WRIG)

**Wound Rotor Induction Generator (WRIG) connected in a wind power plant:**

Wound rotor induction generator (WRIG) is a constant speed generator. The main components of this wind power plant are:

1. Rotor Blades
2. Gear box
3. WRIG
4. Variable resistance
5. Capacitor unit
6. 3-phase transformer
7. Utility grid

The rotor blades are rotated by the wind. WRIG rotates and convert the mechanical energy of rotation into electrical energy. The generated voltage is stepped up by a 3-phase step-up transformer and transfer to the utility grid for distribution. The generator speed is controlled by a variable resistance. Capacitor unit is used to control the fluctuation in the torque and generated power. The Block diagram of WRIG based wind power plant is shown in Fig. 3.16.

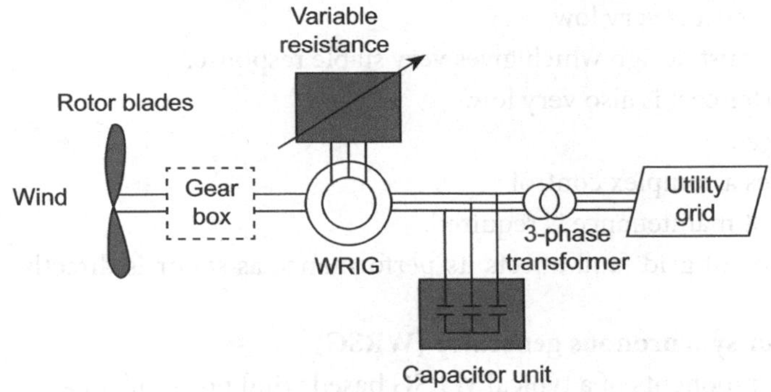


**Fig. 3.16:** Block diagram of WRIG based wind power plant

## 3.6.2 Variable Speed Electric Generators

Variable speed electric generators are designed to operate over a wide range of rotor speed. In these types of wind turbines, the rotor speed varies with the variation in wind speed, in order to capture the maximum power from the wind. Based on the rotor design, there are three types of variable speed electric generator.

**(1) Doubly-fed induction generator (DFIG)**

Followings are the main components of a typical DFIG based wind power plant:

1. Rotor blades
2. Gear box
3. Induction generator
4. Rectifier unit
5. Inverter unit

This generator is suitable for high-capacity power generation applications. In DFIG, the stator winding of generator is directly connected to the utility grid circuit and rotor winding is connected to the grid circuit through rectifier and inverter units. The block diagram of DFIG based wind power plant is shown in Fig. 3.17.

Wind energy received on the turbine blades rotates the shaft of turbine. The rotating shaft rotates the rotor of doubly fed induction generator through gear box. The mechanical power is converted into 3-phase electrical power which feed to the utility grid for further distribution.

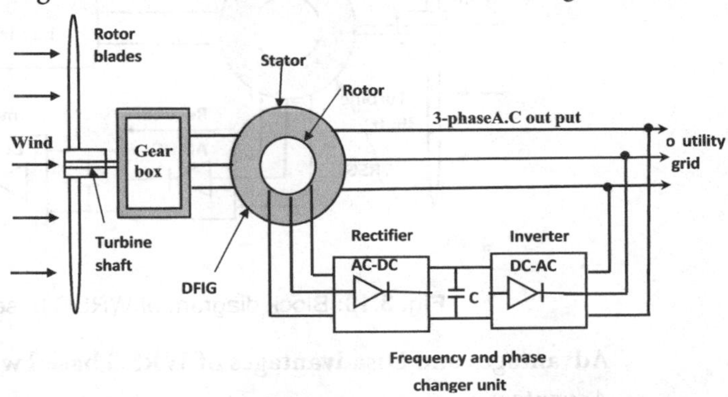


**Fig. 3.17:** Block diagram of DFIG based wind power plant

**Advantages and Disadvantages of DFIG based wind power plant**

*Advantages:*

1. Inverter cost is very low.
2. It is a robust design which gives very stable response.
3. Converter cost is also very low.

*Disadvantages:*

1. Requires a complex control
2. Frequent maintenance is required.
3. Any type of grid fault affects its performance as stator is directly connected to the grid circuit.

**(2) Wound rotor synchronous generator (WRSG)**

The main components of a typical WRSG based wind power plant are:

1. Rotor blade
2. Wound rotor synchronous generator (WRSG)
3. Exciter unit
4. Rectifier unit
5. Inverter unit
6. 3-phase step-up transformer

The block diagram of WRSG based wind power plant is shown in Fig. 3.18. Wind energy received on the turbine blades rotates the shaft of the turbine. The mechanical energy of rotation is converted into electrical power by WRSG. WRSG is connected to a 3-phase transformer through rectifier and inverter units. The voltage is stepped up by this 3-phase step up transformer and power go to the utility grid for further distribution. An exciter is used to excite the wound rotor windings. Rectifier-capacitor-inverter unit is used for back-to-back power conversion.

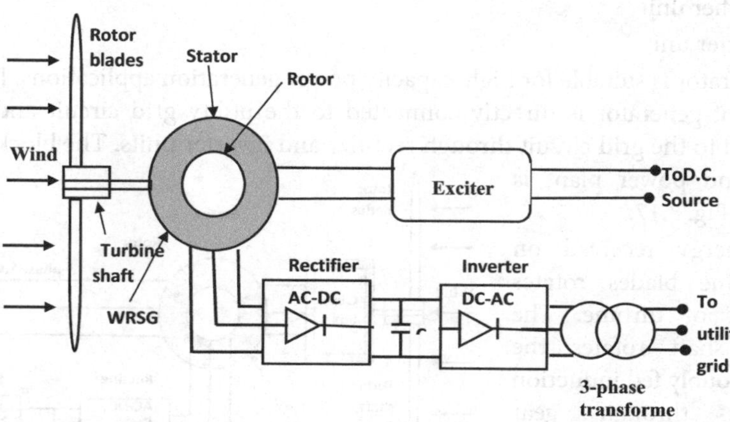


**Fig. 3.18:** Block diagram of WRSG based wind power plant

**Advantages and Disadvantages of WRSG based wind power plant**

*Advantages:*

1. It is suitable for high power generation.

2. Gear box is not required and hence reduces maintenance cost.
3. Stator is not directly connected to the grid hance in case any fault in grid, it can be safe.

*Disadvantages:*

1. An additional D.C source is required
2. Maintenance cost is more.

**(3) Permanent magnet synchronous generator (PMSG)**

The main components of a typical permanent magnet synchronous generator (PMSG) wind power plants are:

1. Rotor blades
2. Turbine shaft
3. Permanent magnet synchronous generator
4. Rectifier unit
5. Inverter unit
6. 3-phase step-up transformer

The block diagram presenting the main components of PMSG based wind power plant is shown in Fig. 3.19.

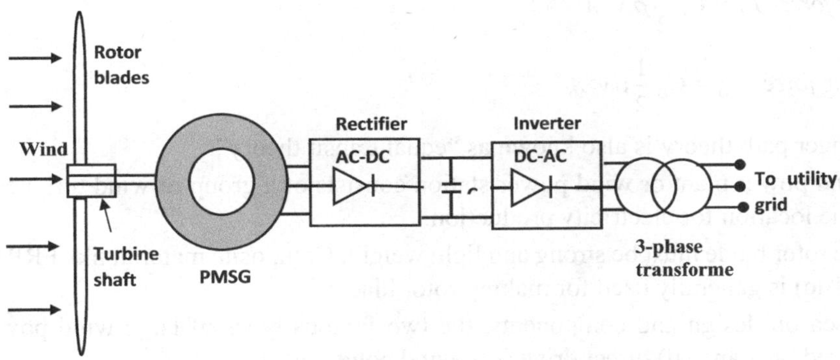


**Fig. 3.19:** Block diagram of PMSG based wind power plant

Wind energy received by the turbine blades rotates the turbine shaft. The rotating shaft rotates the permanent magnet synchronous generator. Mechanical energy associated with the rotation is converted into electrical energy by PMSG. The rectifier converts variable A.C voltage generated by PMSG into D.C voltage. The inverter converts this D.C voltage into a stable A.C voltage which goes to the circuit of utility grid for further distribution. It is useful for small or medium capacity plant.

**Advantages and Disadvantages of PMSG based wind power plant**

*Advantages:*

1. Very simple design and easy to construct.
2. It is cheaper because of no use of gear box.
4. Low maintenance cost.

*Disadvantages:*

1. Chances of de-magnetization of the permanent magnet used in generator.

2. Require arrangement of a cooling system to maintain the temperature.
3. Difficulty of availability of large size of permanent magnet.

## UNIT SUMMARY

- Moving air is called as wind.
- Small wind turbines typically have the power generation capacity below 50 kW.
- Large wind turbines have the generation capacities ranging from 650 kW to 1800 kW.
- Wind power density (WPD) is an indicator for measuring the wind power available at a specific location.
- Most of the states in India have the power density in the range of 0-100 W/m$^2$.
- Device which converts wind energy into electrical energy is known as wind turbine.
- Wind turbine converts the kinetic energy (mechanical energy) of wind into electrical energy.
- The force exerted by the air in the direction of air flow is called as the **drag force.**
- The force exerted in the direction normal to the airflow is called as **lift force**.

  *Lift force* $F_L = C_L \frac{1}{2} \rho . v^2 A$

  *Drag force* $F_D = C_D \frac{1}{2} \rho . v^2 A$

- Longer path theory is also known as "equal transit theory".
- Wind power plant or wind power station consists of a group of wind turbines installed at the same location for electricity production.
- The rotor blade must be strong and light weight. Composite material like FRP (fibre reinforced plastic) is generally used for making rotor blades.
- Based on design and components, the two famous types of large wind power plants are (i) geared type and (ii) direct drive type wind power plant.
- Nacelle consists of components shafts, gear box and generator unit.
- Gear box is placed between rotor blade and generator. It is used to increase the rotational speed of the main shaft connected with electric generator.
- A synchronous generator is made with permanent magnet.
- Rectifier is used to convert AC power generated by generator to the DC power for batteries.
- Inverter converts the D.C power into A.C power which is supplied to the AC load or sent to grid.
- Bed on the system speed, electric generators are classified as:
  (i) Constant Speed Electric generators
  (ii) Variable Speed Electric generators
- Doubly-fed induction generator (DFIG) is suitable for high-capacity power generation applications.

# EXERCISES

## Multiple Choice Questions

1. Wind turbine converts
   (a) chemical energy into mechanical energy
   (b) mechanical energy into electrical energy
   (c) chemical energy into electrical energy
   (d) electrical energy into mechanical energy
2. Wind power density is measured in
   (a) Watt (b) Joule
   (c) Watt/meter$^2$ (d) Watt-sec
3. Most of the states in India have wind power density in the range of
   (a) 0-100 W/m$^2$ (b) 100-200 W/m$^2$
   (c) 200-300 W/m$^2$ (d) 300-400 W/m$^2$
4. Large wind turbines have the generation capacity in the range of
   (a) 100 kW – 500 kW (b) 600 kW-2000 kW
   (c) 50 kW-100 kW (d) 2000 kW – 2500 kW
5. When a body move in air, the force exerted by air in the direction of airflow is called as
   (a) lift (b) friction
   (c) drag (d) gravitational
6. When a body move in air, the force exerted by air in the direction normal to the airflow is called
   (a) lift (b) friction
   (c) drag (d) gravitational
7. The main source of formation of wind is
   (a) uneven land (b) sun
   (c) rain (d) vegetation
8. Height of a tower in wind energy power plant is typically
   (a) 10-20 m (b) 20-30 m
   (c) 50-100 m (d) anything
9. Gear box is present in which type of large wind power plants
   (a) geared type (b) direct drive type
   (c) in both (a) and (b) (d) Neither in (a) nor in (b)
10. Electric generator in wind power plant is used to convert
    (a) electric power into mechanical power
    (b) mechanical power into electric power
    (c) both (a) and (b)
    (d) none of these

11. Wound rotor induction generation (WRIG) is a
    (a) constant speed generator
    (b) variable speed generator
    (c) both (a) and (b)
    (d) none of these
12. The function of rectifier in variable speed electric generator is
    (a) to convert AC voltage to DC voltage
    (b) to convert DC voltage to AC voltage
    (c) to convert AC voltage to AC voltage
    (d) to convert DC voltage to DC voltage
13. Part of the wind power plant consisting of the components like drive train, shafts, gear box and generator is known as
    (a) tower (b) nacelle
    (c) yaw drive (d) foundation
14. End rings are used in which generator
    (a) CSIG (b) WRIG
    (c) DFIG (d) WRSG
15. Exciter unit is used in which generator
    (a) CSIG (b) WRIG
    (c) DFIG (d) WRSG

| Answers of Multiple Choice Questions | | | | | | | |
|---|---|---|---|---|---|---|---|
| 1. (b) | 2. (c) | 3. (a) | 4. (b) | 5. (c) | 6. (a) | 7. (b) | 8. (c) |
| 9. (a) | 10. (b) | 11. (a) | 12. (a) | 13. (b) | 14. (a) | 15. (d) | |

## Short and Long Answer Type Questions

### *Category I*

1. Define wind and wind power density.
2. Define lift and drag forces.
3. What is the use of gear box in wind power plant?
4. Why rectifiers are used in some wind power plants.
5. What is the use of inverter unit in wind power plant?
6. Classify small, medium and large wind power plants on the basic of power generation capacity.
7. Why a variable resistance is required in wound rotor induction generator (WRIG)?

### *Category II*

1. Draw a neat diagram of a wind turbine write the use of various components.
2. Explain longer path theory with the help of a diagram.

3. Explain lift and drag principle of a wind turbine.
4. Differentiate between constant speed and variable speed electric generators.
5. Explain the working of squirrel cage induction generator (SCIG) with the help of a neat diagram.
6. Draw the block diagram of wound rotor synchronous generator (WRSG) and explain its working.

## PRACTICAL

### Identify the routine maintenance parts of the large wind power plant after watching a video programme.

**Aim:**

To identify different parts of large wind power plants for routine maintenance.

**Theory:**

The main components of a wind power plants require routine maintenance are:

- **Rotor blade:** The rotor blade is designed according to the wind speed and the desired power output. The blade must be strong and light weight. Composite material like FRP (fibre reinforced plastic) is generally used for making rotor blades.
- **Gear box:** It is placed between rotor blade and generator. It is used to increase the rotational speed of the main shaft connected with electric generator.
- **Nacelle:** It consists of components shafts, gear box and generator unit.
- **Yaw drive:** It is used to keep the rotor facing the wind direction all the time.
- **Transformer:** Transformer is used to send the electricity produced by wind turbine to the distribution grid. This is a sensitive component of the wind turbine.
- **Tower:** It supports the structure of the turbine. Rotor blades and nacelle are mounted on the top of the tower. Generally, it is made with steel in round tubular shape.
- **Generator:** It is used to convert the rotational energy of the shaft to electrical energy.
- **Foundation:** It is designed to transfer and spread the load of the wind turbine to the soil at depth.

**Routine maintenance of large wind power plant:**

Wind power plant routine maintenance work includes

(1) **Inspection of turbine:** Person who does inspection use various tools and equipment to inspect rotor blades, nacelle, yaw drive, tower and generators. At the time of inspection, they generally take measurement and photos.

(2) **Cleaning of turbine:** It involves removing waste and scarp from blade, nacelle and generator. It can be done manually or with the help of cleaning machine.

(3) **Lubrication of moving parts:** In this, oil and grease are applied in different moving parts of the turbine in order to prevent wear and tear.

(4) **Repair of any fault or damage:** It involves replacing or repairing the damaged part in the turbine.

**Schematic diagram of large wind power plant:**

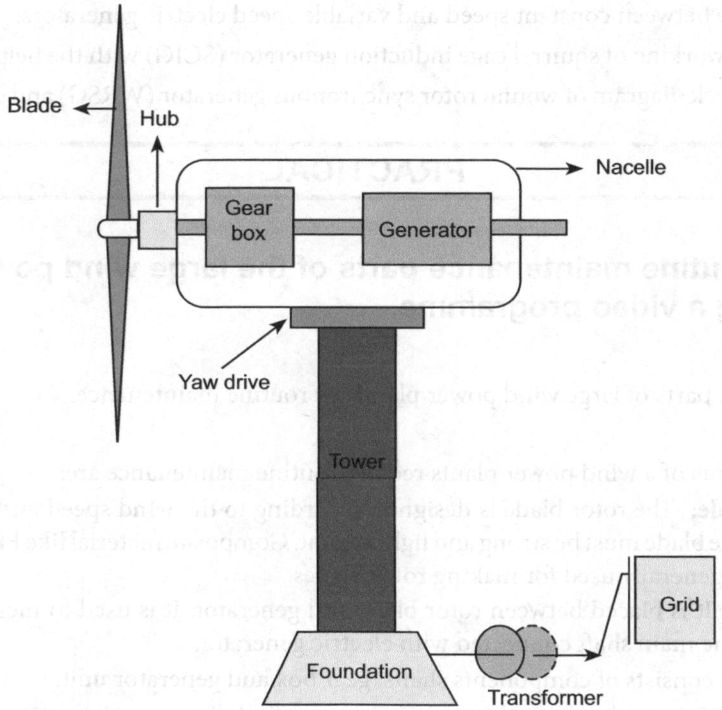


**Fig. (i):** Large wind power plant

**Conclusion:**

In this way we identify the routine maintenance parts of a large wind energy power plant.

## KNOW MORE

**Some interesting facts:**

- Use of wind power is not a new thing. I have been used for thousands of years in some way.
- The first electricity generation wind turbine was constructed in around1888. It had diameter of 17 meters and had 144 blades made from wood. It produced only 12 kW power.
- Wind turbines are not as simple as they look. In fact, a single wind turbine has around 8000 different parts.
- Jiuquan wind power base in China is the world's largest wind power plant with installed capacity of 20 Gigawatt.
- Wind energy is the fastest growing renewable energy source for the countries like US, China and India.

## REFERENCES AND SUGGESTED READINGS


1. J. W. Twidella and A. Weir, *Renewable Energy Sources*, EFN Spon Ltd., UK, 2006.
2. Gipe, Paul: Wind Energy Basics, Chelsea Green Publishing Co; ISBN: 978- 1603580304
3. G. N. Tiwari and R. K. Mishra, *Advanced Renewable Energy Resources*, RSC Publishing, UK, 2012.
4. Rachel, Sthuthi; Earnest, Joshua – Wind Power Technologies, PHI Learning, New Delhi, ISBN:978-93-88028-49- 3; E-book 978-93-88028-50-9
5. N. H. Ravindranath, U. K. Rao, B. Natarajan, P. Monga, *Renewable Energy and Environment-A Policy Analysis for India*, Tata McGraw Hill.
6. R. A. Ristinen and J. J. Kraushaar, *Energy and The Environment, Second Edition*, John Willey & Sons, New York, 2006.
7. D. P. Kothari, *Renewable Energy Sources and Emerging Technologies*, PHI Learning, New Delhi, ISBN: -978-81-203-4470-9.
8. S. N. Bhadra, D. Kastha, S. Banerjee, Wind Electrical Systems installation; Oxford University Press, New Delhi, ISBN: 9780195670936


Dynamic QR Code for Further Reading

# 4 Small Wind Turbines

## UNIT SPECIFICS

Following major points have been discussed in the chapter:

- Types of wind turbines based on the orientation of the turbine axis.
- Direct drive and Geared type horizontal and vertical axis wind turbine
- Various types of wind towers used in small wind turbines
- Different types of electric generators used in small wind turbines

The main components of a typical small wind turbine have been presented in the unit. Types of wind turbine based on the orientation of rotor shaft with ground have been discussed. Working of horizontal and vertical axis wind turbine in geared and direct drive type configurations has also been explained with the help of components wise block diagrams. Various designs of wind towers used in small wind turbines have been discussed in details. Installation process of small wind turbines on roof of a building and in open fields have been given. A discussion of different types of electric generators used in small wind power plants have been presented.

Together with the large and short answer type problems multiple-choice questions have been given for the better understanding of the reader of the book. A list of references and suggested readings are given in the unit so that one can go through them for practice. It is important to note that for getting more information on various topics of interest some QR codes have been provided which can be scanned for relevant supportive knowledge.

## RATIONALE

Based on the power generation capacities and their specific applications, wind turbines are generally classified into two broad categories (i) Large wind turbine and (ii) Small wind turbines. Large wind turbines have the generation capacities ranging from 650 kW to 1800 kW and are deigned to use in electricity generation power plants. Small wind turbines typically have the power generation capacity below 50 kW. These turbines are designed to us in agriculture, residential and some small industrial applications.

## PRE-REQUISITES

Knowledge of properties of wind

## UNIT OUTCOMES

List of outcomes of this unit is as follows:

**U4-O1:** To study about the horizontal and vertical axis wind turbine.

**U4-O2:** To study about geared and direct drive type small wind turbines.

**U4-O3:** To understand the installation process of a small wind turbine.

**U4-O4:** To study about different types of wind towers used in small wind turbines.

**U4-O5:** To study about electric generators used in small wind turbines

| Unit-4 Outcomes | EXPECTED MAPPING WITH COURSE OUTCOMES (1-Weak Correlation; 2-Medium Correlation; 3-Strong Correlation) | | | | |
|---|---|---|---|---|---|
| | CO-1 | CO-2 | CO-3 | CO-4 | CO-5 |
| U4-O1 | - | 3 | 3 | - | - |
| U4-O2 | - | 1 | 3 | - | - |
| U4-O3 | - | 1 | 3 | - | - |
| U4-O4 | - | 2 | 3 | - | - |
| U4-O5 | - | 2 | 3 | - | - |

## 4.1 OVERVIEW

Wind energy is the energy associated with the force of the wind. Wind carries huge amount of energy. Wind energy is now become one of the mostly used renewable energy resources. It has been used for various applications. Increasing price of fossil fuels and environment related problems like climate change and global warming have led to a significant growth in the installation of wind turbines around the world.

Wind turbines are the machines which converts wind energy into electrical energy by using electric generators. Main components of a wind turbine are shown in Fig. 4.1.

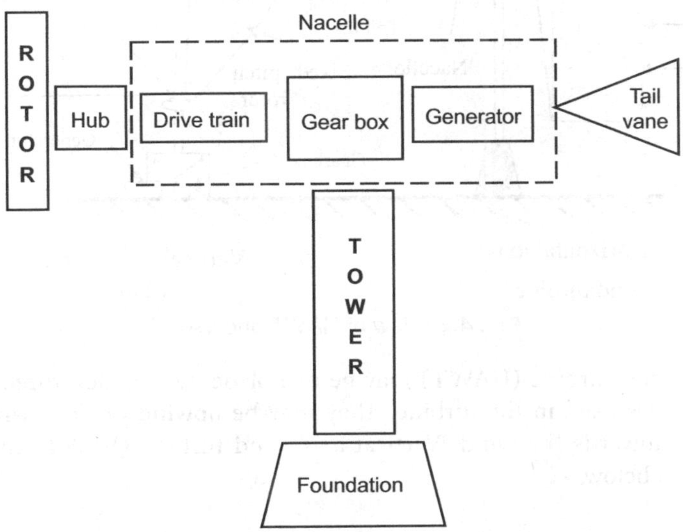


**Fig. 4.1:** Wind turbine components

When wind energy is received by rotor blades, it rotates the rotor shaft and mechanical energy of this rotation is converted into electrical energy by a generator.

Wind turbine exists is various sizes. Some are used for small scale domestic applications like battery charging, water pumping, communications etc. Some others are used in wind power plants for large scale electricity generation as clusters called "wind farms". Turbines used for small scale domestic applications are termed as **small wind turbines**. These turbines are also known as "aerogenerators". The generation capacity of small wind turbines varies between 0.3 to 100 kW. The generated power also depends on the average wind speed at the location. A small wind turbine requires average wind speed of 4 m/s at the height of the turbine. The small wind turbine may be a good option for the rural area that are not still connected to the electric grid.

## 4.2 TYPES OF SMALL WIND TURBINES

According to the orientation of the rotor shaft with ground, small wind turbines can be classified as:

(1) Horizontal axis wind turbine (HAWT)

(2) Vertical axis wind turbine (VAWT)

Horizontal axis wind turbine (HAWT) rotates on horizontal axis and vertical axis wind turbine (VAWT) rotates on vertical axis. Both type of these wind turbine has its merits and demerits. Horizontal axis wind turbine produces more electricity as compared with vertical axis wind turbine for a given amount of wind. The view of HAWT and VAWT is shown in Fig. 4.2.

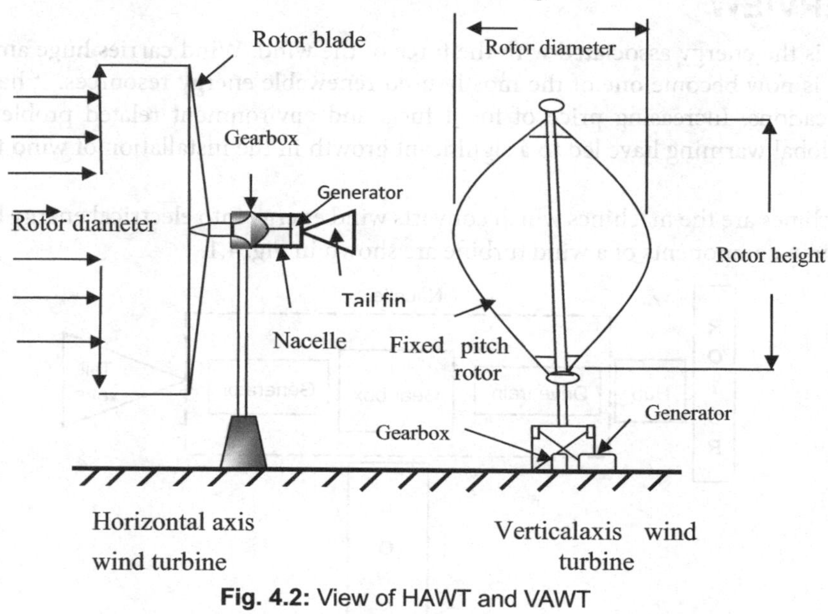


**Fig. 4.2:** View of HAWT and VAWT

Horizontal axis wind turbine (HAWT) may be one blade, two blades, three blades turbine based on the number of blades used in the turbine. They may be upwind or downwind depending on the orientation of blades towards the wind. Vertical axis wind turbine (VAWT) may be Savnious type, darrieus type as shown below.

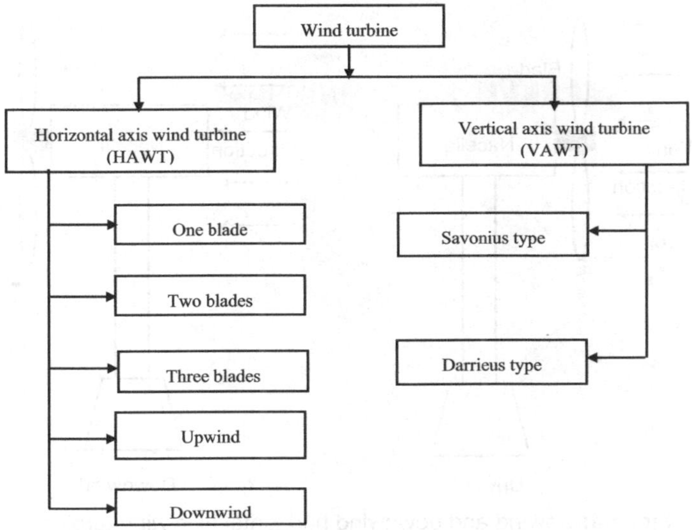


### 4.2.1 Horizontal Axis Wind Turbine (HAWT)

In horizontal axis wind turbine, the axis of rotation of main rotor shaft is parallel to the ground. The rotating blades are placed perpendicular to the ground. Depending on the number of blades present in the rotor, HAWT may be single blade type, double blade and three bladed types. They generally use a tail vane to point blades into the wind. HWAT with one blade, two blade and three blades is shown in Fig. 4.3.

**Fig. 4.3:** HAWT with one blade, two blades and three blades

According to the orientation of blades with respect to the wind, HAWT are also classified as (i) upwind and (ii) downwind type. In upwind type turbines, the wind approaches the blade from front side and nacelle is positioned on the back side of the blade. In downwind type turbines, the wind approaches the blade from the nacelle side. The upwind and downwind horizontal axis wind turbines are shown in Fig. 4.4. Majority of the wind turbines are of upwind design. The main advantage of this over downwind design is that it avoids the wind shade behind the tower.

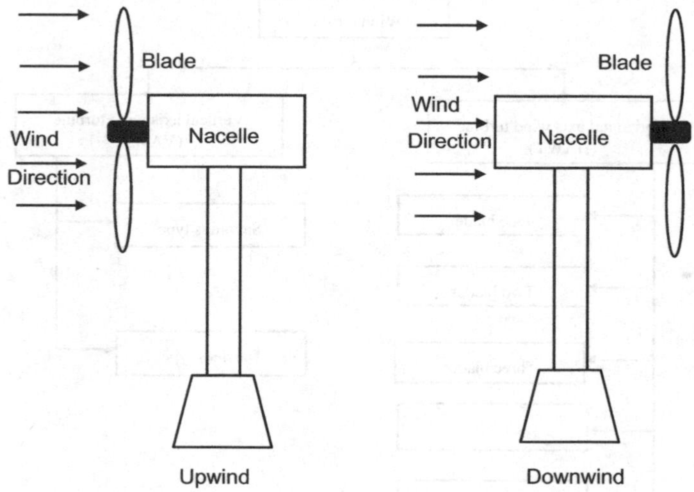


**Fig. 4.4:** Upwind and downwind horizontal axis wind turbine

### 4.2.2 Vertical Axis Wind Turbine (VAWT)

In vertical axis wind turbine, the axis of rotation of rotor shaft is perpendicular to the ground. The rotor shaft is also perpendicular to the direction of the wind. The main components like gear box, generator etc. are placed at the base of the turbine which makes its service and repair easy. Nacelle is not required in VAWT. These turbines are found lighter in weight and cheaper in cost. VAWT are mostly used in small wind industries and residential area. They capture the wind from all directions so no need to be pointed towards the wind. Tall towers and long blades are not required for VAWT. Though the VAWT has many advantages over HAWT but they are less efficient and produces less energy as compared with HAWT.

Vertical axis wind turbines are of two types:

(a) Savonius type

(b) Darrieus type

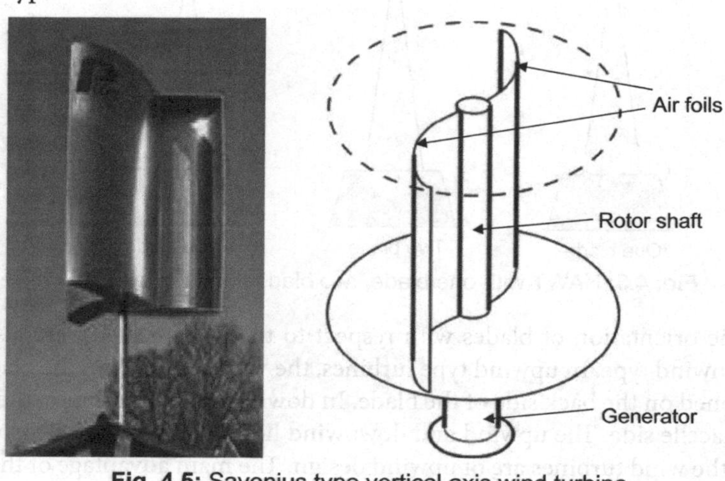


**Fig. 4.5:** Savonius type vertical axis wind turbine

(a) **Savonius type:** It was first invented by a Finnish architect and inventor S.J. Savonius. He got his invention patented in 1929. Savonius rotor consists of two curved metal air foils of S-shape. Air foils are supported by two circular plates from top and bottom. It looks as S-shape if viewed from top. It is drag type VAWT which uses drag force to drive the rotor. It is a slow rotating high torque machine. An actual photograph and schematic diagram of a savonius type VAWT is depicted in Fig. 4.5.

The main advantages of Savonius type turbine are:

(i) It can operate at low wind velocity.

(ii) Yaw control is not required.

(iii) Generator can be placed at the ground.

(iv) Installation cost is low.

(v) Easy to maintain.

Savonius type VAWT are used for the applications like water pumping, grinding of grains etc.

(b) **Darrieus type:** Darrieus type wind turbine is commonly known as **Eggbeater** because of its shape. It consists of two or three curved blades. It is driven by lift force. It was invented by Georges Darrieus in 1931. It is a high speed and low torque machine generally used for generating AC electricity. Initial movements of the blades may require some external power source because starting toque is very low. An actual photograph and schematic diagram of a Darrieus type VAWT is depicted in Fig. 4.6

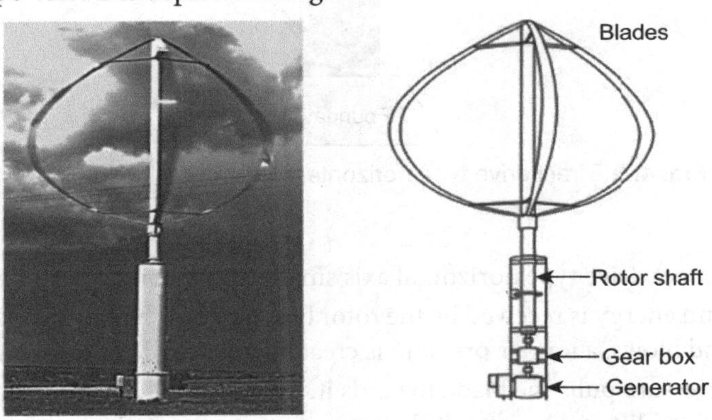


**Fig. 4.6:** Darrieus type vertical axis wind turbine

## 4.2.3 Direct Drive Type Horizontal Axis Small Wind Turbine

Horizontal axis wind turbine without gearbox is known as direct drive type horizontal axis wind turbines.In these turbines, the rotor is directly connected to the generator and no gear box is present in between blade and generator. In these turbines, the generator speed is equal to the rotor speed because rotor is directly connected to the generator. The layout of a direct drive type horizontal axis small wind turbine is shown in Fig. 4.7. Since these turbines do not have gearboxes, the main component is the nacelle is the generator.

Main components of a typical direct drive type horizontal axis small wind turbine are:

1. **Rotor blades:** Turbine blades are made with lightweight materials for better performance.
2. **Rotor hub:** It hold the blades and connect them to the main shaft of the turbine.

3. **Tail vane:** Used to point the blades in the direction of the wind.
4. **Generator:** Generator converts the mechanical power of the shaft into electrical power.
5. **Tower:** It supports the structure of the turbine. Rotor blades and nacelle are mounted on the top of the tower. Generally, it is made with steel in round tubular shape.
6. **Foundation:** It is designed to transfer and spread the load of the wind turbine to the soil at depth.

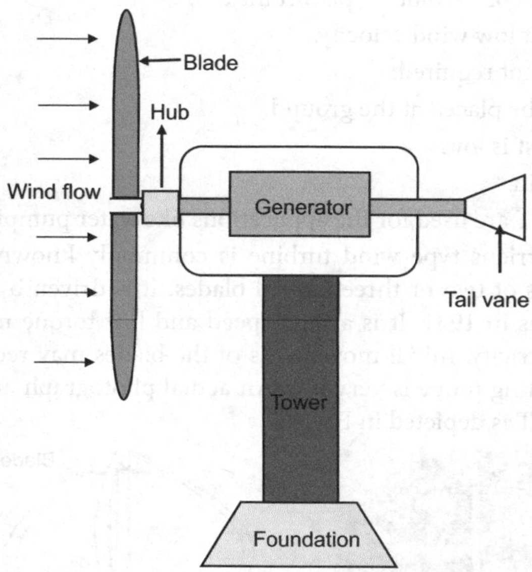


**Fig. 4.7:** Direct drive type horizontal axis small wind turbine

**Working:**

The working of a direct drive type horizontal axis small wind turbine is as follows:

1. Firstly, the wind energy is received by the rotor blades. Rotor blades act like an aeroplane wing. When the wind blows, a low air pressure is created on one side of the blade.
2. This low air pressure pulls the blade towards it. This is called as **"lift"**. Blades are flat in shape which increase the lift and as a result the rotor shaft starts rotating.
3. The force of this lift is much stronger than wind force acting from the front side of the blade which is called as **"drag"**. This combination of lift and drag causes rotor to rotate like a propeller.
4. The kinetic energy of the wind changes into mechanical energy through the revolution of the rotor. This mechanical energy is transmitted through the shaft towards the generator.
5. Finally, the generator converts the mechanical energy into electrical energy to generate electricity.

**Merits and Demerits of Direct Drive Type Horizontal Axis Small Wind Turbine**

*Merits:*

1. These turbines are more efficient than geared type plants.
2. It is more reliable than geared type turbines.
3. It gives better performance
4. Since no gear box needed, it requires less maintenance.

*Demerits:*

1. Transportation problem is more as compared with geared type wind power plant
2. Mechanical and electromagnetic structure need to be improved.

### 4.2.4 Geared Type Horizontal Axis Small Wind Turbine

It is old and complex design of the wind turbine. In this turbine, the rotor blades are connected to the generator through a gearbox which is used to increase the rotation speed of the shaft. The layout of a typical geared type small wind turbine is shown in Fig. 4.8.

Main components of a geared type wind power plant are:

1. **Rotor blade:** The rotor blade is designed according to the wind speed and the desired power output. The blade must be strong and light weight. Composite material like FRP (fibre reinforced plastic) is generally used for making rotor blades.
2. **Hub:** It hold the rotor blade and connect them to the shaft. It must hold the blade in its proper position to get maximum aerodynamic efficiency. It rotates in order to drive the generator.
3. **Gear box:** It is placed between rotor blade and generator. It is used to increase the rotational speed of the main shaft connected with electric generator.
4. **Generator:** It is used to convert the rotational energy of the shaft to electrical energy.
5. **Nacelle:** It consists of components shafts, gear box and generator unit.
6. **Tail vane:** Used to point the blades in the direction of the wind.
7. **Tower:** It supports the structure of the turbine. Rotor blades and nacelle are mounted on the top of the tower. Generally, it is made with steel in round tubular shape.
8. **Foundation:** It is designed to transfer and spread the load of the wind turbine to the soil at depth.

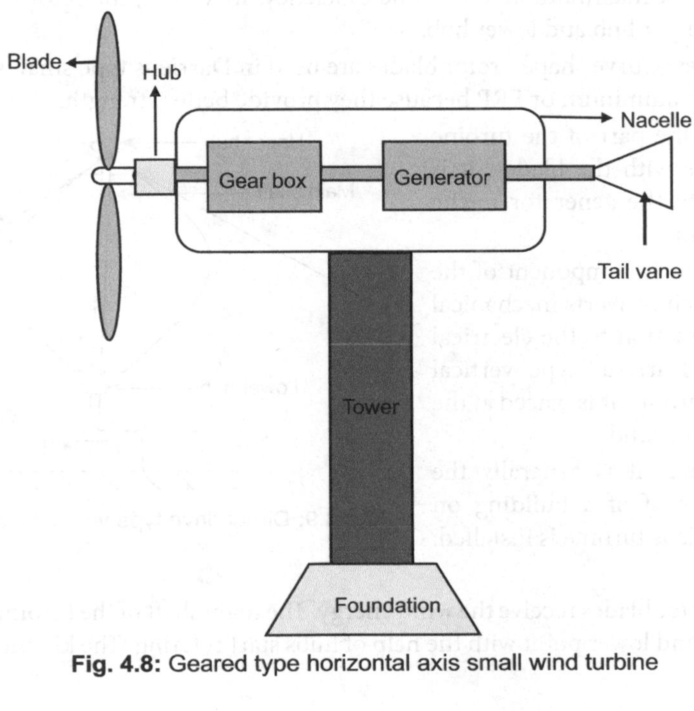


**Fig. 4.8:** Geared type horizontal axis small wind turbine

**Working:**

Wind blows on the rotor blade connected with the shaft. The shaft start rotating because of the combination of lift and drag forces. Rotational speed of the shaft increases up to around 1800 rpm with the help of series of gears present in the gear box. The shaft rotating with high speed drives the generator which produces the electrical energy.

**Meritsand Demeritsof Geared Type Horizontal Axis Small Wind Turbine**

*Merits:*

1. Provides high torque to the shaft
2. Able to provide high speed operation.

*Demerits:*

1. Very old and complicated design
2. Gears causes friction losses up to 10%.
3. High maintenance is required because of so many moving parts.

### 4.2.5 Direct Drive Type Vertical Axis Small Wind Turbine

The main rotor shaft of a vertical axis wind turbine is arranged in the vertical direction to the ground. Generator and other primary parts are placed at the base of the turbine. In direct drive type vertical axis wind turbine rotor shaft is directly connected to the generator without gear box. The layout of typical direct drive Darrieus type vertical axis small wind turbine is shown in Fig. 4.9.

The main components of a Darrieus type small wind turbine are:

1. **Guide wire:** It helps in keeping the rotor shaft vertically in a foxed position.
2. **Hub:** It hold the rotor blade and connect them to the shaft. It must hold the blade in its proper position to get maximum aerodynamic efficiency. In VAWT, the rotor blades are attached at twopoint, upper hub and lower hub.
3. **Rotor blades:** Curve shaped rotor blades are used in Darrieus type small wind turbine. Blades are made up aluminum or FRP because they provide better strength.
4. **Shaft:** It is the part of the turbine which turns with the blades. It is connected to the generator in the main housing.
5. **Generator:** It is component of the turbine which converts mechanical energy of rotation to the electrical energy. In Darrieus type vertical axis wind turbine, it is placed at the base on the ground.
6. **Turbine base:** It is generally the ground or roof of a building on which Darrieus turbine is installed.

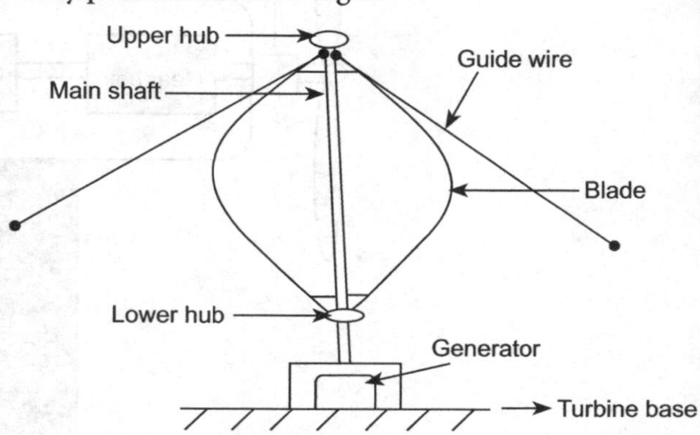


**Fig. 4.9:** Direct drive type vertical axis small wind turbine

**Working:**

When the aero foils rotor blades receive the wind energy. The main shaft of the turbine which is connected to the blade at upper and lower point with the help of hubs start rotating. The kinetic energy is converted into mechanical energy through the shaft. This mechanical energy is then transferred to the generator placed near the base. The generator converts the mechanical energy into electrical energy to produce electricity.

**Merits and Demerits of Direct Drive Type Vertical Axis Small Wind Turbine**

*Merits:*

1. More efficient than geared type wind turbines.
2. It gives better performance
3. Since no gear box needed, it requires less maintenance.

*Demerits:*

1. Transportation problem is more as compared with geared type wind power plant
2. Mechanical and electromagnetic structure need to be improved.

### 4.2.6 Geared Type Vertical Axis Small Wind Turbine

In geared type vertical axis small wind turbine, the main rotor shaft is arranged in the vertical direction. Generator and other primary parts are placed at the base of the turbine. In this design, turbine rotor shaft is connected to the generator through a gear box. The layout of a geared type vertical axis small wind turbine is shown in Fig. 4.10.

The main components of a geared type vertical axis small wind turbine are:

1. **Guide wire:** It helps in keeping the rotor shaft vertically in a foxed position.
2. **Hub:** It hold the rotor blade and connect them to the shaft. It must hold the blade in its proper position to get maximum aerodynamic efficiency. In VAWT, the rotor blades are attached at twopoints, upper hub and lower hub.
3. **Rotor blades:** Curve shaped rotor blades are used in this type of small wind turbine. Blades are made up aluminum or FRP because they provide better strength.
4. **Shaft:** It is the part of the turbine which turns with the blades. It is connected to the generator in the main housing.
5. **Gear box:**Gear box with multiple gears is placed in between rotor blade and generator. It is used to increase the rotational speed of the main shaft connected with the generator. It is placed near the base at ground.
6. **Generator:** It is component of the turbine which converts mechanical energy of rotation to the electrical energy. It is generally placed at the base on the ground.
7. **Turbine base:** It is generally the ground or roof of a building on which turbine is installed.

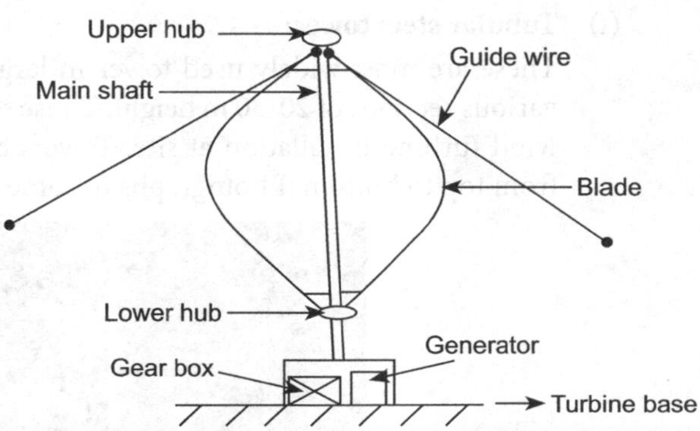


**Fig. 4.10:** Geared typevertical axis small wind turbine

**Working:**

When the rotor blades receive the wind energy then because of lift force, they start spinning around the main shaft. The main shaft of the turbine which is connected to the blade at upper and lower point with the help of hubs start rotating. Rotational speed of the shaft increases with the help of series of gears present in the gear box. The kinetic energy is converted into mechanical energy through the shaft. This mechanical energy is then transferred to the generator placed near the base. The generator converts the mechanical energy into electrical energy to produce electricity.

**Merits and Demerits of Geared Type Vertical Axis Small Wind Turbine**

*Merits:*

1. Provides high torque to the shaft.
2. Able to provide high speed operation.

*Demerits:*

1. Gears causes friction losses.
2. High maintenance is required because of so many moving parts.

## 4.3 WIND TURBINE TOWER

Wind tower is one of the important components of the wind turbine. It transmits the load from nacelle to the foundation of the turbine. The height of the is an important parameter for the energy generation form a wind turbine. It has been observed that high towers produce more energy.

The wind turbine towers are basically of two types:

(1) Self-supporting (free standing) tower

(2) Guyed pole tower

### *(1) Self-supporting towers:*

They are mostly used in large wind turbines. Depending on the shape and materials used in construction of the tower, self-supporting towers may be of different types.

(i) Tubular steel tower

(ii) Lattice tower

(iii) Hybrid tower

**(i) Tubular steel tower:**

These are most widely used tower in large wind turbines. These are fabricated with steel in various sections of 20-30 m height. These sections are joined together with nut and bolts during wind turbine installation at site. Towers are conical in shape with their diameter increasing from top to bottom. Photographs of some tubular steel tower is shown in Fig. 4.11.

Fig. 4.11: Tubular steel tower

**(ii) Lattice tower:**

Lattice towers are made up of welded steel profiles instead of steel sheets. The materials required to manufacture these towers are almost half as required for fabrication of tubular tower of same stiffness. Because of this reason these towers are cheaper than tubular tower. They allow the wind to pass through their sections which decreases the pressure on the turbine structure. One disadvantage of this tower is its appearance. Because of some aesthetic reasons lattice towers are almost disappeared from use. Fig. 4.12 depicts lattice towers.

**(iii) Hybrid tower:**

Hybrid towers made up of steel and concrete are used to fabricate tall towers. Bottom section is made up of concreter which provides heavy base and protection from corrosion. The upper section is made up of tubular steel. Steel-concrete hybrid tower is depicted in Fig. 4.13.

**Fig. 4.12:** Lattice tower

**Fig. 4.13:** Steel hybrid tower

### *(2) Guyed pole tower:*

Guyed pole towers are mainly used in small wind turbines. These towers are fabricated with narrow pole which are supported by guy wires. They are lighter in weight and also have low cost. Guyed pole towers are easier to install as compared with self-supporting towers. The disadvantage of guyed pole towers is the difficulty in accessing the apace around the tower.

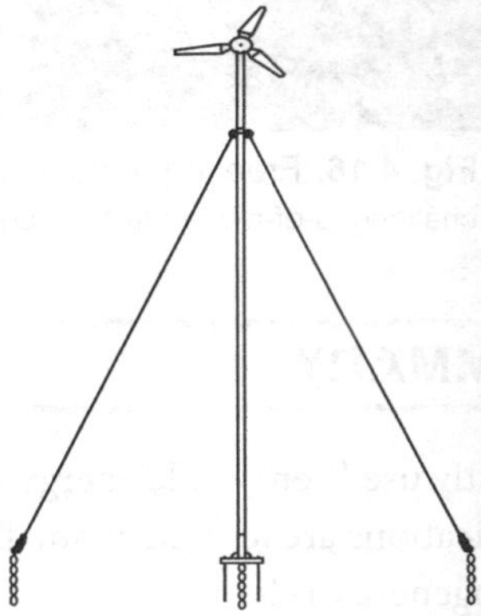

**Fig. 4.14:** Guyed pole tower

## 4.4 SMALL WIND TURBINE INSTALLATION

The small wind turbines used for residential purposes generally ranges from 400 watts to 20 kilowatts. They generally have three blades with a typical rotor diameter of about 15 feet. The blades are mounted on a 40 to 100 feet tall tower. Smaller wind turbines are used to store energy in batteries and to generate electricity for individual houses and business park or corporate buildings. Small wind turbines can be placed on the roof of a building or can also be installed in an open filed in some specific locations.

Rooftop mounted wind turbines can be suitable to generate electricity up to 2 kW. Installation of small wind turbine of the rooftop of a building make sense only if we install the turbine high enough in the location where no barriers or obstacles affect the wind patterns. Living in a windy area also helps. Before going for installation of rooftop wind turbine first one has to determine the its suitability.

Getting electricity from renewable sources like solar panels and wind turbines is exciting but at the same time if these systems are installed under the wrong conditions, the system may not meet our expectations. It has been observed that rooftop small wind turbines might work effectively if installed under following conditions:

- Installed in an area with high or frequent winds
- House must be in an open area and not close to trees and other structures.
- House is in an area that is far from the electrical grid.
- Can install the turbine high in the air.

For rural area with few trees and houses surrounding the house, a rooftop wind turbine will be more effective than the big city or towns. Also, for the houses which cannot be easily connected to the grid or grid connection is expensive, rooftop wind turbine could be a good option. Photographs of a rooftop and free standing small wind turbines are shown in Fig. 4.15 and 4.16 respectively.

**Fig. 4.15:** Rooftop small wind turbine

**Fig. 4.16:** Free standing small wind turbine

(**Source:** https://undecidedmf.com/episodes/the-challenges-of-a-wind-turbine-on-your-home/)

## UNIT SUMMARY

- Wind energy is now become one of the mostly used renewable energy resources.
- Turbines used for small scale domestic applications are termed as small wind turbines.
- Small wind turbines are also known as "aerogenerators".

- The generation capacity of small wind turbines varies between 0.3 to 100 kW.
- The small wind turbine may be a good option for the rural area that are not still connected to the electric grid.
- According to the orientation of the rotor shaft with ground, small wind turbines can be classified as:
  (1) Horizontal axis wind turbine (HAWT)
  (2) Vertical axis wind turbine (VAWT)
- In horizontal axis wind turbine, the axis of rotation of main rotor shaft is parallel to the ground.
- Horizontal axis wind turbine (HAWT) may be one blade, two blades, three blades turbine based on the number of blades used in the turbine.
- In vertical axis wind turbine, the axis of rotation of rotor shaft is perpendicular to the ground.
- Vertical axis wind turbine (VAWT) may be Savnious type or darrieus type.
- Savnious type turbine was first invented by a Finnish architect and inventor S.J. Savonius. He got his invention patented in 1929.
- Darrieus type wind turbine is commonly known as Eggbeater because of its shape. It was invented by Georges Darrieus in 1931.
- Horizontal axis wind turbine without gearbox is known as direct drive type horizontal axis wind turbines. In these turbines, the rotor is directly connected to the generator and no gear box is present in between blade and generator.
- In geared type turbine, the rotor blades are connected to the generator through a gearbox. It is old and complex design of the wind turbine. Gears are used to increase the rotation speed of the shaft.
- Wind tower is one of the important components of the wind turbine. It transmits the load from nacelle to the foundation of the turbine.
- The wind turbine towers are basically of two types:
  (1) Self-supporting (free standing) tower
  (2) Guyed pole tower
- Self-supporting (free standing) tower are mostly used in large wind turbines.
- Guyed pole towers are mainly used in small wind turbines. These towers are fabricated with narrow pole which are supported by guy wires.

## EXERCISES

### Multiple Choice Questions

1. The generation capacity of small wind turbines varies between
   (a) 300 to 3000 kW (b) 0.3 to 100 kW
   (c) 30 to 300 kW (d) 3 to 30 Megawatts
2. The average wind speed required for small wind turbine at the height of the turbine is
   (a) 1 m/s (b) 2 m/s
   (c) 3 m/s (d) 4 m/s

**3.** **Which of the following is the correct order of the components arranged in a wind turbine for energy conversion**

(a) blade – rotor – generator - shaft

(b) blade – rotor – shaft - generator

(c) shaft – blade – rotor - generator

(d) generator – blade – rotor - shaft

**4.** **What abbreviation VAWT is generally used for**

(a) variable area wind turbine

(b) volt ampere wind turbine

(c) variable axis wind turbine

(d) vertical axis wind turbine

**5.** **Which is true for a horizontal axis wind turbine**

(a) the axis of rotation of main rotor shaft is perpendicular to the plan of ground

(b) the axis of rotation of main rotor shaft is diagonal to the plane of ground

(c) the axis of rotation of main rotor shaft is about 30 degrees to the plane of ground

(d) the axis of rotation of main rotor shaft is parallel to the plane of ground

**6.** Which is true for a vertical axis wind turbine

(a) the axis of rotation of main rotor shaft is perpendicular to the plane of ground

(b) the axis of rotation of main rotor shaft is diagonal to the plane of ground

(c) the axis of rotation of main rotor shaft is about 30 degrees to the plane of ground

(d) the axis of rotation of main rotor shaft is parallel to the plane of ground

**7.** What is an upwind

(a) rotor of the turbine is behind the unit

(b) rotor of the turbine is in front of the unit

(c) rotor is positioned at the bottom of the tower

(d) rotor is positioned at the center of the tower

**8.** The main advantage of an upwind turbine is

(a) increased tower shadow effect

(b) reduced tower shadow effect

(c) no tower shadow effect

(d) manufacturing

**9.** What is a downwind turbine?

(a) rotor is positioned at the three-quarters of the height of the tower

(b) rotor of the turbine is in front of the unit

(c) rotor is positioned at the bottom of the tower

(d) rotor of the turbine is behind the unit

**10.** Gear box is present in which type of small wind turibe

(a) geared type (b) direct drive type

(c) in both (a) and (b) (d) Neither in (a) nor in (b)

11. Based on the type of rotor, one of the vertical axis wind turbines is
    (a) propeller type (b) wound rotor type
    (c) savonius type (d) multiple blade type
12. Which turbine is also known as Eggbeater
    (a) Darrieus type (b) Savonius type
    (c) propeller type (d) wound rotor type
13. The wind tower suitable for large wind power plants is
    (a) Self-supporting (free standing) tower
    (b) Guyed pole tower
    (c) both (a) and (b)
    (d) None of these
13. The component used to point the blades in the direction of the wind is
    (a) rotor shaft (b) tail vane
    (c) yaw drive (d) foundation
14. Guyed pole towers are mainly used in small wind turbines
    (a) large wind turbine (b) small wind turbines
    (c) both (a) and (b) (d) none of these
15. Component used for transmitting the load from nacelle to the foundation of the turbine is
    (a) tower (b) rotor shaft
    (c) transformer (d) generator

| Answers of Multiple Choice Questions | | | | | | | |
|---|---|---|---|---|---|---|---|
| 1. (b) | 2. (d) | 3. (b) | 4. (d) | 5. (d) | 6. (a) | 7. (b) | 8. (b) |
| 9. (d) | 10. (a) | 11. (c) | 12. (a) | 13. (b) | 14. (b) | 15. (a) | |

## Short and Long Answer Type Questions

### *Category I*

1. What is the use of tail vane in small wind turbines?
3. What is geared type horizontal axis wind turbine.
4. What are different types of vertical axis wind turbine.
3. Name different types of towers used in small wind turbines.
5. Which type of turbine is preferred for water pumping and grinding of grains.

### *Category II*

1. What is vertical axis wind turbine. Explain Darrieus type and Savonius type vertical axis wind turbine.
2. Differentiate between horizontal and vertical axis wind turbine.
3. Explain the working of geared type horizontal axis wind turbine with the help of a diagram. Also mentions some of its advantage and disadvantage.

4. Explain the working of direct drive type horizontal axis wind turbine with the help of a neat diagram.
5. Explain different designs of towers used in small wind turbines. Also discuss advantages and disadvantage of each.

## PRACTICAL

## Assemble a horizontal axis small wind turbine to produce electric power

**Aim:**

To assemble the horizontal axis small wind turbine to produce electric power.

**Theory:**

The assembly of a horizontal axis wind turbine can be done by connecting various components of the turbine. The horizontal axis wind turbine components mainly include:

- **Rotor blade:** The rotor blade is designed according to the wind speed and the desired power output. The blade must be strong and light weight. Composite material like FRP (fibre reinforced plastic) is generally used for making rotor blades.
- **Nacelle:** It consists of components shafts, gear box and generator unit.
- **Tower:** It supports the structure of the turbine. Rotor blades and nacelle are mounted on the top of the tower. Generally, it is made with steel in round tubular shape.
- **Generator:** It is used to convert the rotational energy of the shaft to electrical energy.
- **Tail vane:** It is used to turn the rotor into direction of the wind.
- **Foundation:** It is designed to transfer and spread the load of the wind turbine to the soil at depth.

**Schematic diagram of a horizontal axis small wind turbine:**

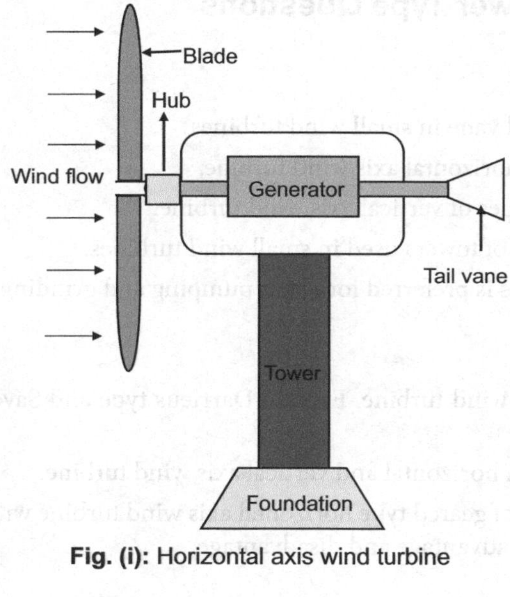


**Fig. (i):** Horizontal axis wind turbine

Assembling of a horizontal axis wind turbine can be done in the following steps:

1. **Foundation preparation and installation:** Depending on the size of the turbine it may require some machines like cranes. We need to wait for 1-2 weeks after laying of foundation to allow concrete base to cure. In case of roof mounted turbine, it is necessary to have the roof strengthened in order to bear the weight of the turbine.
2. **Digging of trenches:** Trenches need to be dug for the electrical cables from the turbine to the control unit and inverter.
3. **Fixing of tower and turbine:** The tower needs to be fixed on the foundation and the components like blade, generator need to be installed on the top of the tower.
4. **Electrical wiring:**The wind turbine DC output is connected to the control box and then to the inverter. The AC output from the inverter is then connected to the households for end use.
5. **Final checks:** The system finally need to checked for electrical safety and performance before commissioning the system.

**Conclusion:**

In this way one can assemble a horizontal axis small wind turbine.

## REFERENCES AND SUGGESTED READINGS


1. J. W. Twidella and A. Weir, *Renewable Energy Sources*, EFN Spon Ltd., UK, 2006.
2. Gipe, Paul: Wind Energy Basics, Chelsea Green Publishing Co; ISBN: 978- 1603580304
3. G. N. Tiwari and R. K. Mishra, *Advanced Renewable Energy Resources,* RSC Publishing, UK, 2012.
4. Rachel, Sthuthi; Earnest, Joshua – Wind Power Technologies, PHI Learning, New Delhi, ISBN:978-93-88028-49- 3; E-book 978-93-88028-50-9
5. N. H. Ravindranath, U. K. Rao, B. Natarajan, P. Monga, *Renewable Energy and Environment-A Policy Analysis for India*, Tata McGraw Hill.
6. R. A. Ristinen and J. J. Kraushaar, *Energy and The Environment, Second Edition*, John Willey & Sons, New York, 2006.
7. D. P. Kothari, *Renewable Energy Sources and Emerging Technologies*, PHI Learning, New Delhi, ISBN: -978-81-203-4470-9.
8. S. N. Bhadra, D. Kastha, S. Banerjee, Wind Electrical Systems installation; Oxford University Press, New Delhi, ISBN: 9780195670936


Dynamic QR Code for Further Reading

# 5 Micro-Hydro Power Plants

## UNIT SPECIFICS

Following major points have been discussed in the chapter:

- Energy conversion process using hydro power plants
- Various types of hydro power plants: High, medium and low head hydro power plants
- Design and working of hydro turbines used in hydro power plants
- Safe practices for micro hydro power plants

The energy conversion process using hydro power plants has been presented in the unit. Classification of various types of hydropower plants based on head height, power generation capacity and source of water used have also been discussed. Construction and working of high head, medium head and low head (i.e., micro hydro) power plants is presented in detailed manner. Different types of hydro turbines used in micro hydro power plants are also discussed. Some of the safe practices for the people working at hydro power stations are presented in the unit.

Together with the large and short answer type problems, multiple-choice questions have been given for the better understanding of the reader of the book. A list of references and suggested readings are given in the unit so that one can go through them for practice. It is important to note that for getting more information on various topics of interest some QR codes have been provided which can be scanned for relevant supportive knowledge.

## RATIONALE

Hydro power plants can be categorized based on their power generation capacities. The smallest plants with power generation capacity between 1 to 100 kW are called as micro-hydropower plants. Plants with capacity between 100 kW to 1 MW are known as mini-hydropower plants. One with generation capacity ranging between 1 MW to 10 MW is known as small-hydropower plant and plants with capacity larger than 10 MW are classified as large hydropower plants.

## PRE-REQUISITES

Basic idea about various form of energy (Class X)

## UNIT OUTCOMES

List of outcomes of this unit is as follows:

**U5-O1:** To understand the energy conversion process in hydro power plants.

**U5-O2:** To learn about different types of hydropower plants.
**U5-O3:** To study about the working of hydro turbines used in hydro power plants.
**U5-O4:** To understand the layout of micro hydro power plants.
**U5-O5:** To learn about the safe practices regarding micro hydro power plants

| Unit-5 Outcomes | EXPECTED MAPPING WITH COURSE OUTCOMES (1-Weak Correlation; 2-Medium Correlation; 3-Strong Correlation) | | | | |
|---|---|---|---|---|---|
| | CO-1 | CO-2 | CO-3 | CO-4 | CO-5 |
| U5-O1 | - | - | - | 3 | - |
| U5-O2 | - | - | - | 3 | - |
| U5-O3 | - | - | - | 3 | - |
| U5-O4 | - | - | - | 3 | - |
| U5-O5 | - | - | - | 3 | - |

## 5.1 HYDROPOWER PLANTS

Hydropower (or water power) is an ancient well known renewable source of energy which use potential energy of falling or fast running water to produce electricity. It is one of the oldest and widely used form of renewable energy. Water is first stored in a reservoir at some height behind a dam and then the water is allowed to flow downwardsthrough the water channel. The potential energy of water in the dam is thus converted into kinetic energy. The fast-moving water flows from dam to the turbine placed at the bottom. This fast-moving water starts rotating the blades of turbine. A shaft in between the turbine connects a mechanical generator which converts the mechanical energy of rotation into electricity. Electricity being generated by generator is then distributed through the transmission lines to the end users.

The flow of energy conversion process can be represented as:

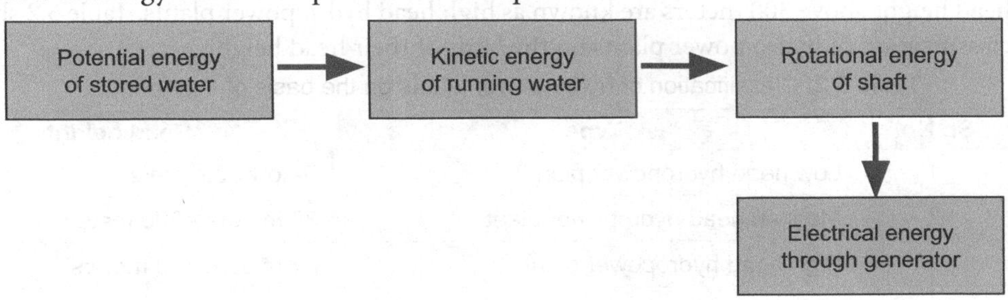


Hydro power plants can be categorized based on their power generation capacities. The smallest plants with power generation capacity between 1 to 100 kW are called as micro-hydropower plants. Plants with capacity between 100 kW to 1 MW are known as mini-hydropower plants. One with generation capacity ranging between 1 MW to 10 MW is known as small-hydropower plant and plants with capacity larger than 10 MW are classified as large hydropower plants. (Source: UNDP/World)

## 5.2 CLASSIFICATION OF HYDRO POWER PLANTS

Based on technology and applications, hydropower plants are broadly classified into three groups. They are classified based on their size, head and source of water.

(a) **Classification based on capacity of power generation (Size):** Based on the power generation capacity, hydro power plants can be classified as micro, mini, small and large hydro power plants. Micro hydro power plants have the generation capacity between 1 to 100 kW. Mini hydro power plants have generation capacity between 100 kW to 1 MW. The plants with generation capacity ranging between 1 MW to 10 MW are known as small-hydropower plant and plants with capacity larger than 10 MW are classified as large hydropower plants. Table 5.1 shows the classification of hydro power plants on the basis of their size.

**Table 5.1:** Classification of hydro power plants on the basis of their size

| Sr. No. | Type | Generation capacity | Uses |
|---|---|---|---|
| 1 | Micro-hydro power plant | 1 - 15 kW | Usually provided power for small community |
| 2 | Mini-hydro power plant | 100 kW- 1 MW | Either used as stand alone or more often feeding into the electricity grid |
| 3 | Small-hydro power plant | 1 MW – 10 MW | Usually feeding into electricity grid |
| 4 | Large-hydro power plant | > 10 MW | Feeding into a large electricity grid |

(b) **Classification based on head:** Head is defined as the height difference between inlet and outlet levels of water in a hydro power plant. Head tells us about the pressure of water (Pressure head=fluid pressure/(acc. due to gravity x density of fluid) falling on the turbine which in turn decide the output power generated by the power plant. Head is an important parameter in the design of a hydro power plant. On the basis of head, hydro power plants are classified as low head, medium head and high head hydro power plants. There is not a specific standard head height for the classification based on head and it may have different values for different countries. In general, low head hydro power plants have head height below 30 meters, medium head hydro power plants have head height between 30 meters to 300 meters and plants having head height above 300 meters are known as high head hydro power plants. Table 5.2 shows the classification of hydro power plants on the basis of their head height.

**Table 5.2:** Classification of hydro power plants on the basis of their head

| Sr. No. | Type | Head height |
|---|---|---|
| 1 | Low head hydropower plant | Below 30 meters |
| 2 | Medium head hydropower plant | 30 meters - 300 meters |
| 3 | High head hydropower plant | More than 300 meters |

(c) **Classification based on source of water:** Based on source of water used, hydro power plants can be classified into following three types:

(i) Running river, in which the natural flow of river or drop in water height is used to generate electricity.

(ii) Storage hydro power, where water is stored behind a dam and the potential energy of the water is used to generate electricity.

(iii) Pumped storage hydro power, in which water is first pumped from a lower source to higher source by using pump in off-peak hour. Then the potential energy of water at higher source is used to generate electricity.

Classification of hydropower plants based on the source of water is presented in Table 5.3.

**Table 5.3:** Classification of hydro power plants on the basis of source of water

| Sr. No. | Type | Source of water |
|---|---|---|
| 1 | Running river | Uses natural flow of river |
| 2 | Storage hydropower plant | Water is stored behind a dam |
| 3 | Storage pumped hydropower plant | Water is first pumped from a lower source to higher source and then potential energy of water is used for electricity generation |

The block diagram of various types of hydro power plants is shown in Fig. 5.1.

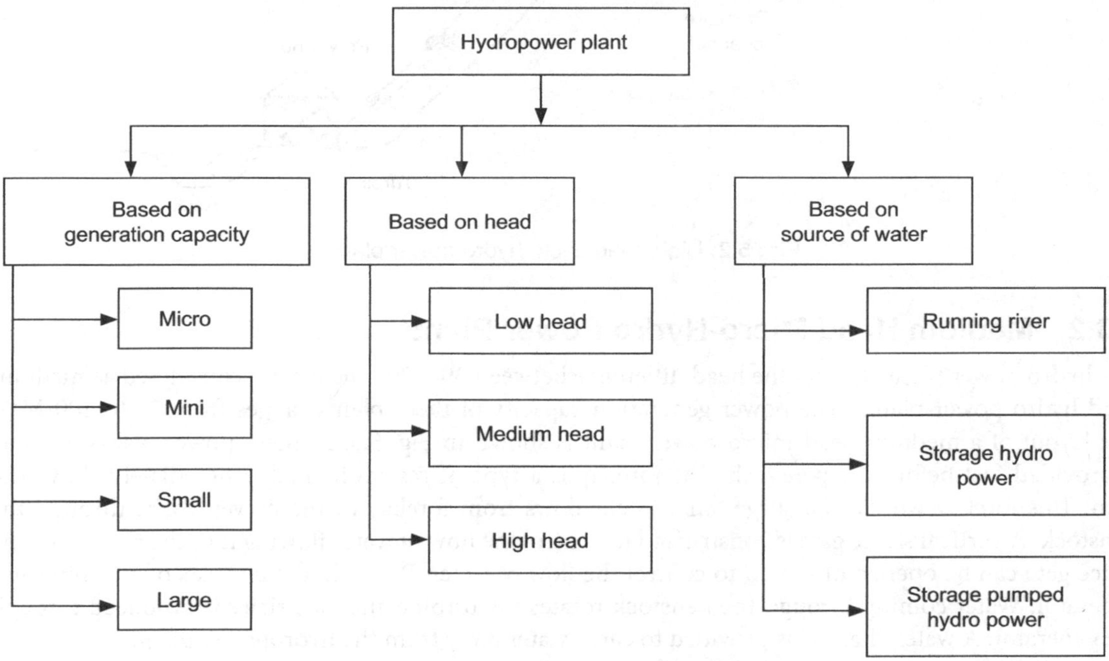


**Fig. 5.1:** Block diagram of various types of hydro power plants

## 5.3 HIGH, MEDIUM AND LOW HEAD MICRO-HYDRO POWER PLANTS

Micro hydro power plants have the generation capacity of up to 100 kilowatts. These plants are generally used to produce electricity for a single home and farm. Based on the height of water and water head, micro-hydro power plants are divided into three categories:

### 5.3.1 High Head Micro-Hydro Power Plant:

High head micro-hydro power plants have the head difference of 300 meters or higher. A dam of such height is constructed to reserve the water in the reservoir. From reservoir, water travel through a pressure channel which is connected to the valve house. A connecting pipe known as penstock which is made up of huge steel pipe is used to supply the water from valve house to the turbine. The power house consists of a turbine and the generator. The potential energy of water in the reservoir is converted into kinetic energy as it flows through the penstock. Water falling from the reservoir through penstock spins the blade of the turbine. The rotation of the turbine is used to run the generator in the power house and finally electrical energy is produced. The layout of a high head micro power plant is shown in Fig. 5.2.

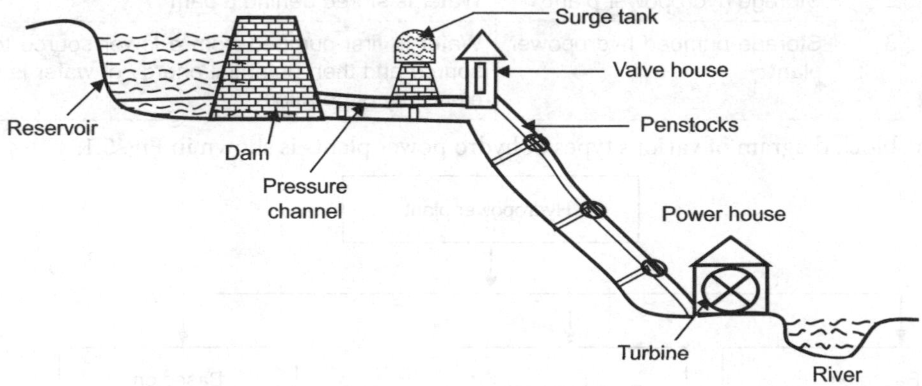


**Fig. 5.2:** High head micro hydro power plant

## 5.3.2 Medium Head Micro-Hydro Power Plant

The hydro power plants having the head difference between 30 – 300 meters are considered as medium head hydro power plants. The power generation capacity of these plants ranges from 25 to 100 MW. The layout of a medium head micro power plant is shown in Fig. 5.3. In these power plants, forebay is provided just before the penstock. The forebay is a type of reservoir made immediately above the dam. This forebay works as a surge tank. Water flows from forebay to the power house through the penstock. A vertical sluice gate is constructed to control the flow of water flowing into the penstock. The sluice gate can be opened or closed to control the flow of water. Power house consists of a turbine and generator. Water coming through the penstock rotates the turbine and electricity is produced through the generator. A water channel is provided to carry water away from the hydropower plant.

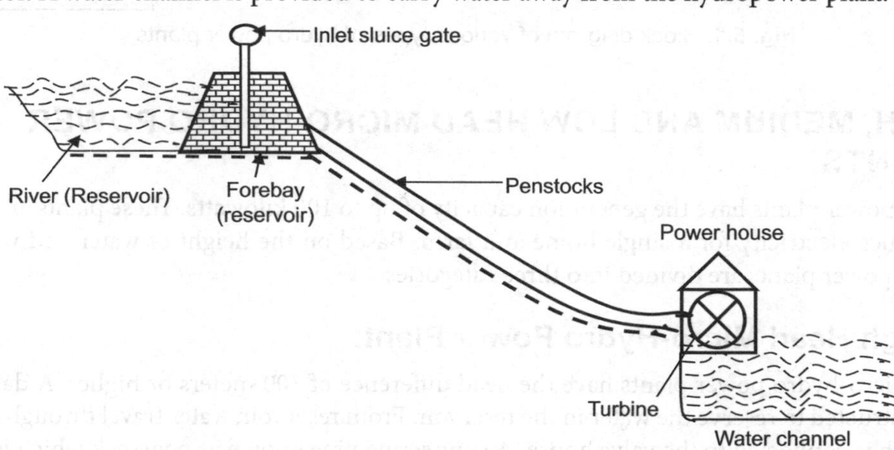


**Fig. 5.3:** Medium head micro hydro power plant

### 5.3.3 Low Head Micro-Hydro Power Plant

In low head hydropower plants, a small dam is constructed across the river itself for providing the necessary water head. The head height in these plants is kept below 30 meters. The excess water is allowed to flow over the dam. No surge gate is required in these plants. The production of electricity is very less because of low head.

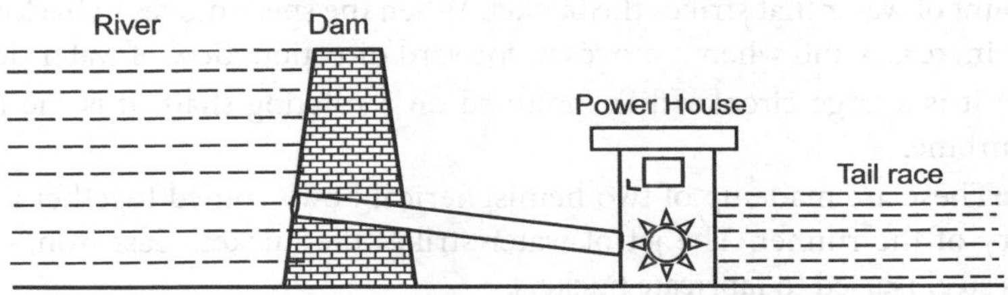


**Fig. 5.4:** Low head micro hydro power plant

## 5.4 HYDROTURBINES

Hydro turbine is a machine which converts kinetic energy of the flowing water into mechanical energy in the form of rotation. Because of the use of water, these turbines are also known as water turbines. Based on the type of energy at the inlet to the turbine, mainly two types of turbines are used in hydropower plants, i.e., reaction turbine and impulse turbine. The selection of hydro turbine used in a particular hydro power plant also depends on the water head and flow of water over the time. A block diagram showing different types of turbines is presented in Fig. 5.5.

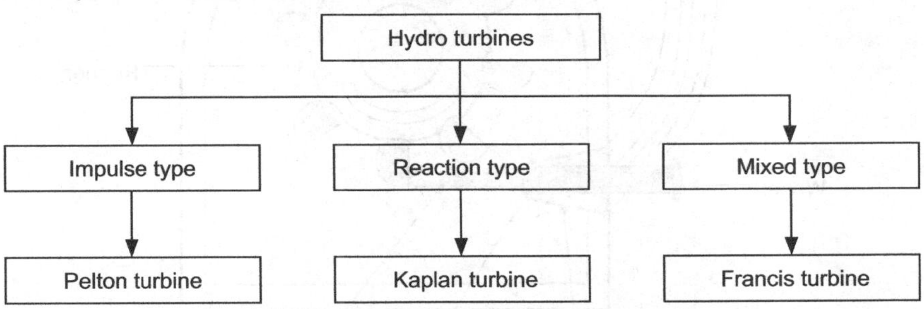


**Fig. 5.5:** Block diagram of various types of hydro turbines

Based on the head under which turbine has to work in a hydro power plant, different types of water turbines are used:

### 5.4.1 Pelton Turbine

Pelton turbine also known as Pelton wheel is a type of impulse turbine. These are used in high head hydro power plants where the head height is greater than 300 meters. This turbine was first designed by an American engineer Lester Pelton in 1880. In high head hydropower plant, the fast-moving water strikes the Pelton turbine and it extracts energy from the impulse of moving water by slowing the flow of water down. The actual photograph of a typical Pelton turbine is shown in Fig. 5.6.

**Fig. 5.6:** Pelton turbine

**Construction of Pelton Turbine:**

The layout of Pelton turbine showing various main components is shown in Fig. 5.7. The main components of Pelton turbine are:

(1) **Nozzle and Spear:** A nozzle is used to increase the kinetic energy of the coming water from reservoir through penstock. A spear is a conical needle installed inside the nozzle which controls the amount of water that strikes the bucket. When the spear moves in backward direction, flow of water increases and when it moves in forward direction, flow of water decreases.

(2) **Runner:** It is a large circular disk mounted on a rotating shaft. It is the rotating part of the Pelton turbine.

(3) **Buckets:**These are made up of two hemispherical bowls joined together and are fixed on the periphery of the runner. The jet of water strikes the bucket. Cast iron, cast steel bronze or stainless steel is used to fabricate buckets.

(4) **Breaking jet:** A small nozzle directed towards the back of the bucket is provided to stop the runner. This jet is called as breaking jet.

(5) **Casing:** Casing is the outer covering of the turbine. It is made up of cast iron or fabricated steel plates. It prevents the splashing of water and also helps to discharge the water to the trail race.

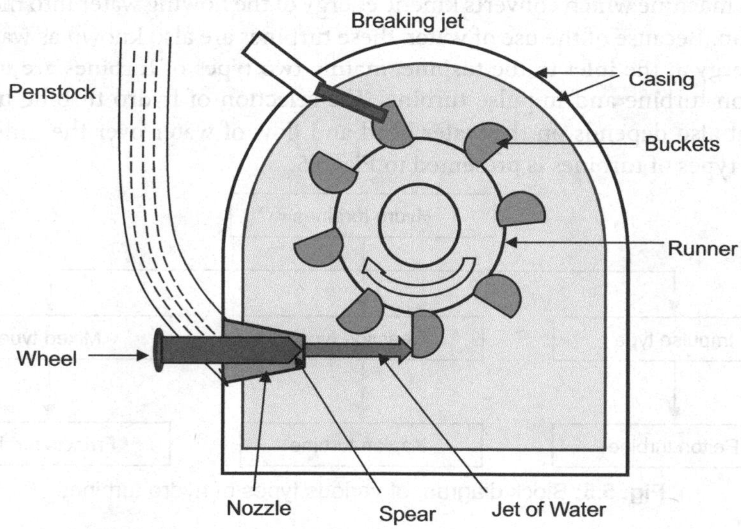


**Fig. 5.7:** Layout of Pelton turbine

**Working of Pelton turbine:**Water stored in the reservoir of the high head micro power plant allowed to flow through the penstock and reaches to the nozzle of the Pelton turbine. Nozzle increases the kinetic energy of the flowing water and ejects the water in the form of a jet. The jet of water then strike the bucket which is fixed on the runner with very high speed. Spear is used to control the amount of water striking the bucket. A mechanical generator is attached to the rotating shaft of the turbine which converts the rotation energy of the runner into electricity.

## 5.4.2 Francis Turbine

Francis turbine is the combination of both impulse and reaction turbines. It is also known as mixed flow turbine as it works on two flow patterns namely radial and axial flow patterns. Water enters radially into the runner and leaves axially. It is mostly used in medium head hydro power plants where the head height is between 30 – 300 meters. It was invented by an American civil engineer James B. Francis. A picture of a typical Francis turbine is shown in Fig. 5.8.

**Construction of Francis turbine:**

The main parts of the Francis turbine are:

(1) **Spiral case:** Water coming from the reservoir through the penstock enters to the turbine via the spiral case. It works as the inlet for the water to the turbine. Water from the reservoir is allowed to pass through this case with high pressure. Turbine blades are circular and hence water striking the turbine blades should flow in circular axis.

**Fig. 5.8:** Francis turbine

(2) **Stationary vanes:** It always remains stationary at their position. It reduces the swirling of water due to radial flow when water enters the runner blades.

(3) **Guided vanes:** Guided vanes change their angles to control the angle of striking of water to the turbine blades. They also regulate the flow rate of water into the runner and controls the power generated by the turbine.

(4) **Runner:** The efficiency and power output from the Francis turbine is strongly dependent on the design of runner. In this turbine, runner is divided into two parts. The lower part is made up in the shape of small bucket and uses the impulse action of water to rotate the turbine. The upper part uses the reaction force of water flowing through the turbine. These two forces make the runner to rotate.

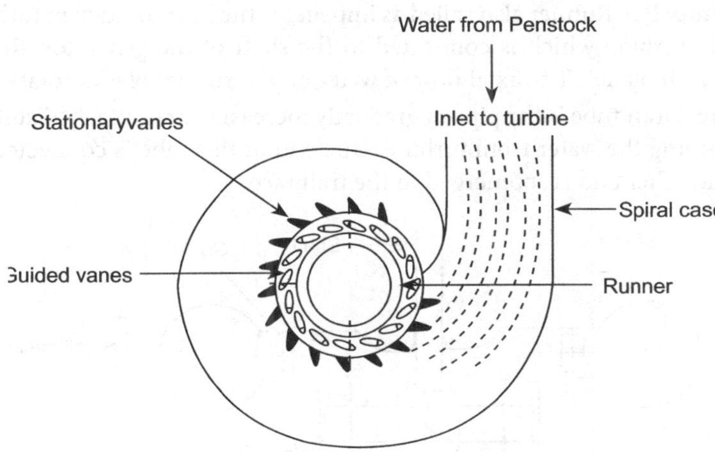


**Fig. 5.9:** Layout of Francis turbine

**Working of Francis Turbine:**

The water coming from the reservoir through penstock enters to the spiral case. Spiral case allows water to flow towards stationary and guided vanes. The diameter of spiral case gradually decreases to maintain the flow pressure. The design of spiral case is such that water strikes each blade of turbine at constant speed. Turbine blades are mounted on the runner. Runner blades are divided into two parts. The lower part is made in the shape of small bucket and uses the impulse action of water to rotate the turbine. The upper part uses the reaction force of water flowing through the turbine. These two forces make the runner to rotate. The shaft of the runner is connected to a mechanical generator where the rotational energy of the runner is converted into electricity.

### 5.4.3 Kaplan Turbine

Kaplan turbine is a reaction type turbine which is widely used in low head hydropower plants where head height is below 30 meters. These turbines are smaller in size and easy to construct. It was invented by Austrian Professor Viktor Kaplan in 1913. Kaplan turbines have adjustable blades and change their location to get maximum efficiency in different water supply conditions. Picture of a Kaplan turbine is shown in Fig. 5.10.

**Construction of KaplanTurbine:**

The layout of a Kaplan turbine is shown in Fig. 5.11. It has following major components:

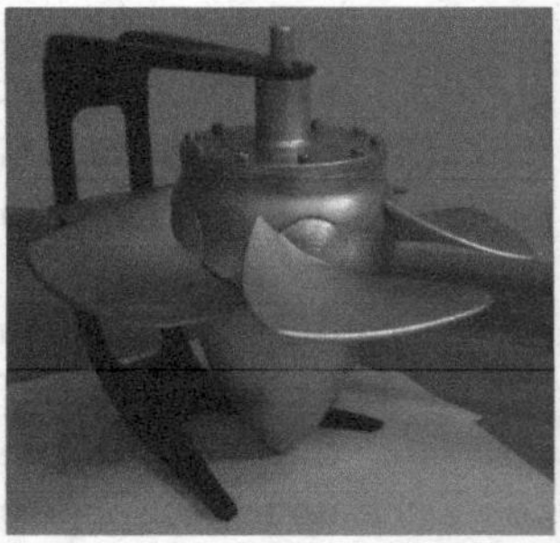

**Fig. 5.10:** Kaplan turbine

(1) **Scroll casing:**It is fabricated in spiral shape with decreasing cross sectional area. It provides a covering to the guide vane. Water coming from penstock first enters into the scroll casing. From scroll casing water goes to the guide vane where it turns through $90^0$ from and flows axially over the runner blade.

(2) **Guide vane:** It is the controlling part of the Kaplan turbine. It opens and closes based on the energy demand. In case of more energy demand, it opens more and allows more water to flow towards the runner blades.

(3) **Runner/Impeller:**Runner also called as impeller is the heart of Kaplan turbine. It is the rotating part of the turbine which is connected to the shaft of the generator. Runner has large boss mounted with blades. The axial flow of water on the runner blades rotates the shaft.

(4) **Draft tube:** Draft tube is the pipe of gradually increasing area attached at the exit of the turbine for discharging the water from turbine. One end of this tube is connected to the outlet of the runner and other end is submerged in the trail race.

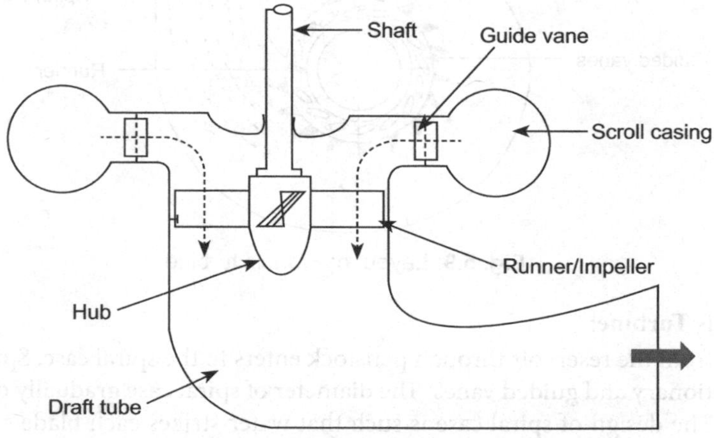


**Fig. 5.11:** Layout of Kaplan turbine

**Working of Kaplan Turbine:**

Water coming from the penstock is allowed to enter to the scroll casing. From scroll casing water goes to the guide vane where it turns through $90^0$ from and flows axially over the runner blade. The runner blades start rotating as the water strikes because of reaction force. From the runner blades water flows into the draft tube and its kinetic energy decreases. The rotation of the turbine is used to rotate the shaft connected with the generator. The rotational energy of the shaft is finally converted into electricity.

## 5.5 SAFE PRACTICES FOR MICRO-HYDROPOWER PLANTS

Micro-hydropower stations can cause significant safety risks for people working there. Micro- hydropower plant owners need to take care of all the possible safety practices concerned with the health and safety at the workplace. Some of the general safety practices for micro-hydropower plants are as follows:

1. **Designing safety:** While designing a new power plant or upgrading an existing power plant one need to consider the required standard of the health and safety.
2. **Planning ahead to control risks:** It is a general approach to minimize the workplace risks like accidents, injuries and illnesses. This can be done by ensuring that systems of work are safe and equipment is properly maintained. All the employees must be well aware with the safety information, training and appropriate supervision.
3. **Safety upgrades for older hydropower plants:** New plants are generally designed by considering appropriate safety measures. While older plants were not often designed regarding safety and may need urgent attention to upgrade those with the required safety standard of the workplace.
4. **Urgent evacuation:** In case of any kind of natural crisis people working at plants must be able to get out of the power station safely. For this hydropower plants must have proper equipment at site.
5. **Flood protection:** Failure of drainage pumps in the power plants may lead to the increase in the water level and eventually can be changed into flood. Water level, flood and evacuation alarms must be installed in the micro-hydropower plants.
6. **Fire and smoke control:** Fires should be detected as early as possible to prevent them from spreading. Smoke control and ventilation are very important and need to be taken care of in all micro-hydropower plants.

## UNIT SUMMARY

- Hydropower which is also known as 'water power' uses potential energy of falling or fast running water to produce electricity.
- The smallest plants with power generation capacity between 1 to 100 kW are called as micro-hydropower plants.
- Micro hydropower plants are generally used to produce electricity for a single home and farm.
- Plants with capacity between 100 kW to 1 MW is known as mini-hydropower plants.
- Plants with generation capacity ranging between 1 MW to 10 MW is known as small-hydropower plant
- Plants with capacity larger than 10 MW are classified as large hydropower plants.

- Low head hydro power plants have head height below 30 meters,
- Medium head hydro power plants have head height between 30 meters to 300 meters
- Plants having head height above 300 meters are known as high head hydro power plants.
- In Run of river type plants, the natural flow of river or drop in water height is used to generate electricity.
- In storage hydro power, water is stored behind a dam and the potential energy of the water is used to generate electricity.
- In pumped storage hydro power, water is first pumped from a lower source to higher source by using pump in off-peak hour. Then the potential energy of water in higher source is used to generate electricity
- The power generation capacity of medium head hydro power plants ranges from 25 to 100 MW.
- Hydro turbine is a machine which converts kinetic energy of the flowing water into mechanical energy in the form of rotation.
- The selection of hydro turbine used in a particular hydro power plant also depends on the water head and flow of water over the time.
- Pelton turbine also known as Pelton wheel is a type of impulse turbine.
- Pelton turbine was first designed by an American engineer Lester Pelton in 1880.
- Francis turbine is a combination of both impulse and reaction turbines.
- Francis turbine was invented by an American civil engineer James B. Francis.
- Kaplan turbine is a reaction type turbine which is widely used in low head hydropower plants where head height is below 30 meters.
- Kaplan turbine was invented by Austrian professor Viktor Kaplan in 1913.

## EXERCISES

### Multiple Choice Questions

1. Hydropower is a
   (a) non-renewable source of energy (b) renewable source of energy
   (c) Both (a) and (b) (d) none of these
2. Micro-hydropower plants have the power generation capacity
   (a) 1 kW – 100 kW (b) 100 kW – 1 MW
   (c) 1 MW – 10 MW (d) more than 10 MW
3. Mini – hydro power plants have the power generation capacity
   (a) 1 kW – 100 kW (b) 100 kW – 1 MW
   (c) 1 MW – 10 MW (d) more than 10 MW
4. Small – hydro power plants have the power generation capacity
   (a) 1 kW – 100 kW (b) 100 kW – 1 MW
   (c) 1 MW – 10 MW (d) more than 10 MW

5. Large-hydro power plants have the power generation capacity
   (a) 1 kW – 100 kW  (b) 100 kW – 1 MW
   (c) 1 MW – 10 MW  (d) more than 10 MW
6. High head hydro power plants have the head height of
   (a) 1 – 10 meters  (b) 2 – 50 meters
   (c) less than 100 meters  (d) more than 300 meters
7. Forebay is required in which type of hydro power plant
   (a) low head hydro power plant  (b) medium head hydro power plant
   (c) high head hydro power plant  (d) none of these
8. Pelton turbine is used in
   (a) low head hydro power plant  (b) medium head hydro power plant
   (c) high head hydro power plant  (d) All of these
9. Adjustable blades are used in
   (a) Pelton turbine  (b) Kaplan turbine
   (c) Francis turbine  (d) Reaction turbine
10. Hydro turbine is a machine which converts
    (a) mechanical energy into chemical energy
    (b) kinetic energy into mechanical energy
    (c) kinetic energy into chemical energy
    (d) chemical energy into mechanical anergy

| Answers of Multiple Choice Questions | | | | |
|---|---|---|---|---|
| 1. (b) | 2. (a) | 3. (b) | 4. (c) | 5. (d) |
| 6. (d) | 7. (b) | 8. (c) | 9. (b) | 10. (b) |

## Short and Long Answer Type Questions

### *Category I*

1. Define hydro turbine.
2. Define micro hydro power plants.
3. What are the main application of Kaplan turbine?
4. Differentiate between impulse and reaction turbine.
5. Discuss the use of breaking jet in Pelton turbine.
6. Why draft tube is used in Kaplan turbine?

### *Category II*

1. Discuss the classification of hydro power plants on the basis of head height.
2. Draw the layout of Pelton turbine showing the main parts of it. Also discuss how it works.
3. With the help of a neat diagram explain the working of Kaplan turbine.
4. Explain the construction and working of a Francis turbine.

## PRACTICAL

# Identify the routine maintenance parts of the micro hydro power plantafter watchinga video programme.

**Aim:**

To identify different parts of a large head micro hydro power plant.

**Theory:**

The schematic layout of a typical large head power plant is shown in Fig. (i). The main parts of a large head hydro power plants are:

(1) **Dam/Barrage:** Dam is one of the visible parts of the hydro power plant. It is the place where water is stored and releases in a controlled way through the gates.

(2) **Pressure channels:** Water from reservoir is allowed to flow through this pressure channel. Its length can vary from a few meters to several kilometers depending on the location of the plant.

(3) **Surge tank:** It is storage tank made between dam and valve house and is used to reduce the water pressure during acceleration of large water masses.

(4) **Valve house:** It is the component of hydro power plant where the various valves are used to control amount and water going to penstock. When the valve is fully opened, water flows freely to the penstock and when closed slightly less amount of water will be allowed to flow through the penstock.

(5) **Penstock:** Penstockis a large pipe linked between reservoir to the turbine. They are fabricated by steel. Grates and filters are also attached at the ends of penstock to stop large debris.

(6) **Power house:** It is the house consisting of hydraulic and electrical components like turbine and mechanical generator.

(7) **Turbine:** Turbine is the component where, kinetic energy of rushing water coming from reservoir through penstock is converted into electricity.

(8) **Tailrace:** Tailrace is a water channel containing trail water used to carry water from the power plant. The water coming in this channel has already been used to run the turbine and leaves power generation unit.

**Schematic diagram a large head micro hydro power plant:**

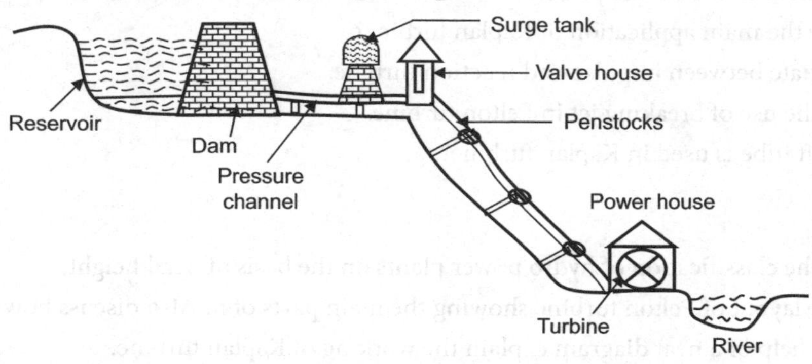


**Fig. (i):** Schematic diagram of a large head micro hydro power plant

**Routine maintenance of hydro power plants:**

One whole day is generally required for hydropower service technicians to complete the maintenance work like:

- Turbine check and inspection
- Turbine bearing inspection and lubrication
- Inspection of gear boxes
- Gear box oil inspection and oil change if required
- Drive belt inspection and replacement if required
- Generator inspection
- Lubrication of the generator bearing
- Hydraulic system inspection
- Hydraulic system oil inspection and oil change if required
- Checking for all the sensors for their correct operation
- Checking for all the controllers for the correct function
- Inspection of inlet area, structures, gates, pipe lines etc.

**Conclusion:**

In this way one can identify and perform the routine maintenance of a hydropower plant.

## REFERENCES AND SUGGESTED READINGS

1. J. W. Twidella and A. Weir, *Renewable Energy Sources*, EFN Spon Ltd., UK, 2006.
2. Gipe, Paul: Wind Energy Basics, Chelsea Green Publishing Co; ISBN: 978- 1603580304
3. G. N. Tiwari and R. K. Mishra, *Advanced Renewable Energy Resources,* RSC Publishing, UK, 2012.
4. N. H. Ravindranath, U. K. Rao, B. Natarajan, P. Monga, *Renewable Energy and Environment-A Policy Analysis for India*, Tata McGraw Hill.
5. R. A. Ristinen and J. J. Kraushaar, *Energy and The Environment, Second Edition*, John Willey & Sons, New York, 2006.
6. D. P. Kothari, *Renewable Energy Sources and Emerging Technologies*, PHI Learning, New Delhi, ISBN: -978-81-203-4470-9.

Dynamic QR Code for Further Reading

# 6 Biomass-Based Power Plants

## UNIT SPECIFICS

Following major points have been discussed in the chapter:

- Properties of solid, liquid and gaseous fuel used for power generation
- Bio-chemical based (e. g. biogas) power plants
- Thermo-chemical based (e. g. municipal waste) power plants
- Agro-chemical based (e. g. bio-diesel) power plants

In this unit, the properties of various solid, liquid and gaseous fuels like bagasse, wood chips, rice husk, municipal waste, Jatropha etc. used for electricity generation has been introduced. The process bio-chemical conversion of electricity from biogas has been discussed. Layout and process of energy conversion through thermo-chemical and agro-chemical based power plant are discussed in the unit.

Large answer type, short answer type and multiple-choice questions are given for better understanding of the readers. A list of references and suggested readings are given in the unit so that one can go through them for practice. It is important to note that for getting more information on various topics of interest some QR codes have been provided which can be scanned for relevant supportive knowledge.

## RATIONALE

India produces huge amount of biomass through municipal waste, agriculture and forestry operations. Around 500 million tons of biomass are generated every year in India. A portion of this is used as fodder and fuel in rural area. Around 150 -200 million tons of biomass is available for electricity generation every year. This amount of biomass is sufficient enough to produce 15000 – 25000 MW of electrical power. Also, the biomass grown on wastelands, sides of roads and railways tracks can be used to generate electricity. As per an estimate the total electricity generation from biomass in India is about 70000 MW.

## PRE-REQUISITES

Knowledge of various forms of energy (Class X)

## UNIT OUTCOMES

List of outcomes of this unit is as follows:

**U6-O1:** To understand the properties of solid fuels used in biomass power plants.

**U6-O2:** To understand the properties of liquid fuels used in biomass power plants.

**U6-O3:** To study a bio-chemical based power plant.

**U6-O4:** To study a thermo-chemical-based power plant.

**U6-O5:** To study an agro-chemical based power plant.

| Unit-6 Outcomes | EXPECTED MAPPING WITH COURSE OUTCOMES (1-Weak Correlation; 2-Medium Correlation; 3-Strong Correlation) | | | | |
|---|---|---|---|---|---|
| | CO-1 | CO-2 | CO-3 | CO-4 | CO-5 |
| U6-O1 | - | - | - | - | 3 |
| U6-O2 | - | - | - | - | 3 |
| U6-O3 | - | - | - | - | 3 |
| U6-O4 | - | - | - | - | 3 |
| U6-O5 | - | - | - | - | 3 |

## 6.1 BIOMASS AND BIOFUELS

The term "bio" is derived from the Greek word "*bios*" meaning life.Biomass is a renewable source of energy. It is an organic matter which comes from the living organisms like plants and animals. Biomass is derived from the plants, forest and mill residues, agriculture crops and wastes, kitchen wastes, wood and wood waste, animal waste, aquatic plants, municipal and industrial waste etc. Biomass in general is produced as a result of the photosynthesis process. It is the process used by plants and other organisms to convert light energy of the sun into chemical energy. In this process the carbon dioxide ($CO_2$) and water ($H_2O$) combines together in presence of sun light and converted into an organic compound called biomass. The photosynthesis reaction can be represented as:

$$6CO_2 + 6H_2O + \text{light} \rightarrow C_6H_{12}O_6 + 6O_2$$

The amount of biomass that can be obtained during the photosynthesis process depends on the availability of sunlight which drives the conversion of $CO_2$ and $H_2O$ into biomass. Biomass used for the production of energy comes from different types of biomass energy resources. The energy derived from biomass is called as biomass energy or **biofuels.**

## 6.2 BIOMASS ENERGY RESOURCES

Based on the material state, biomass energy resources can be classified as:

(1) **Agriculture Products:**This includes wood(s), bagasse plant(s) leaves, husks, plant roots and stems etc. These are the non-edible stalk materials left after the harvest of edible parts of the crops like corn, wheat, grains and sugar cane. The advantages of these type of biomass resources are that they do not require the use of additional land space as they are grown together with the food crops.

(2) **Food Processing Waste:** These are the wastes obtained from the industrial processing of the food products ranging from breakfast and cereal bar manufacturers to fresh and frozen food items and alcohol breweries. These wastes are generally in the form of dry solids or watery liquids. Ethanol is produced after the food processing of these wastes.

(3) **Micipal Solid Waste:** These are the waste items thrown away in garbage bags and are collected by dustbin men. Municipal wastes like metallic and plastic items are not suitable as biomass resources. However, solid wastes like paper, cardboard, discarded food products are attractive sources of endless biomass energy resource.

(4) **Animal Waste:** Biomass energy resources coming from domestic farms, ranches, slaughterhouses, fisheries and dairies which produce huge amount of manure. Liquid sewage, animal waste and also human waste from urban area provides a constant source of chemical energy and gases which can be converted into electrical energy at waste water treatment plants. The treatment of animal waste produces methane and biogas which are used for heating, cooking and transportation.

Various biomass energy resources are presented in Fig. 6.1.

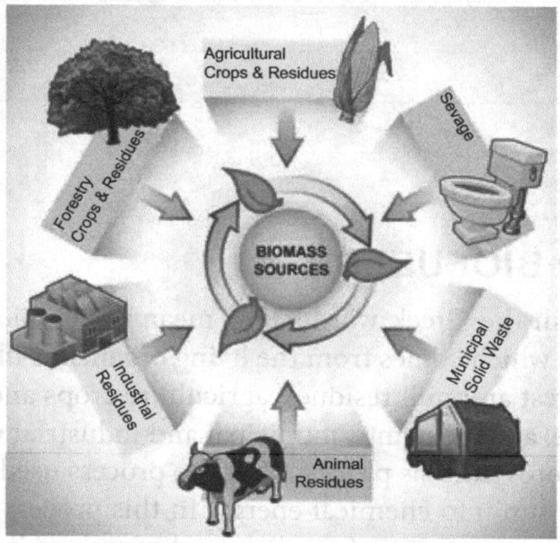


**Fig 6.1:** Biomass energy resources

## 6.3 PROPERTIES OF BIOMASS ENERGY RESOURCES

The main constituents of biomassenergy resource are (i) Lignin (ii) Hemicelluloses (iii) Cellulose (iv) Mineral matter and (v) Ash.

Wood is a solid lignocellulosic material produced in trees and some shrubs. It generally contains 40-50% cellulose, 20-30% hemicelluloses and 20 – 30% lignin. Evaluation of biomass resources as potential energy feedstock generally requires information about their composition, heating value, production yields (in the case of energy crops) and bulk density.

Compositional detailsof any biomass can be presentedwith thehelpof methods like: biochemical analysis, proximate analysis and ultimate analysis.

### 6.3.1 Biochemical Analysis

Biochemical analysis gives us an idea about types and amounts of proteins, oils, sugar, starches and lignocelluloses (Fibre) present in the biomass resource. The biochemical composition of different types of biomasses is presented in Table 6.1 and 6.2. Cellulose is the carbohydrate that is the principal constituent of wood and other biomass. It is a polymer of glucose with a repeating unit of $C_6H_{10}O_5$. It forms the skeletal structure of the plant cell wall. Hemicellulose consists of short, highly branched chains of sugars and is a polymer of five different sugars. Lignin is a non-carbohydrate constituent of wood and other plant material that encrusts the cell walls and cements the cells together. Lignocellulose refers to plant materials made up primarily of lignin, cellulose and hemicelluloses. Herbaceous plants are generally non-woody species of vegetation, usually of low lignin content such as grasses.

**Table 6.1:** Biochemical composition of cellulosic biomass

| Feedstock | Cellulose | Hemicellulose | Lignin |
|---|---|---|---|
| Bagasse | 35 | 25 | 20 |
| Com cobs | 32 | 44 | 13 |
| Wheat straw | 38 | 36 | 16 |
| Short rotation woody crops | 50 | 23 | 22 |
| Herbaceous energy crops | 45 | 30 | 15 |
| Waste paper | 76 | 13 | 11 |

**Table 6.2:** Biochemical composition of starch and sugar biomass

| Feedstock | Protein | Oil | Starch | Sugar | Fibre |
|---|---|---|---|---|---|
| Corn grain | 10 | 5 | 20 | < 1 | 13 |
| Wheat grain | 14 | < 1 | 13 | < 1 | 5 |
| Sugar cane | < 1 | < 1 | < 1 | 50 | 50 |
| Sweet Sorghum | <1 | <1 | <1 | 50 | 50 |

### 6.3.2 Proximate Analysis

Proximate analysis reports the yields (% mass basis) of various products obtained upon heating of biomass under controlled conditions and it helps in developing thermochemical conversion processes for biomass. These products include moisture, volatile matter, fixed carbon and ash. Since the moisture content of biomass is so variable and can be easily determined by gravimetric methods (weighing, heating at 100°C and reweighing), the proximate analysis of biomass is commonly reported on a dry basis. Volatile matter is the fraction of biomass that decomposes and escapes as gases upon heating a sample at moderate temperatures (about 400°C) in an inert (non-oxidizing) environment. Knowledge of volatile material is important in designing burners and gasifiers for biomass. The remaining fraction is a mixture of solid carbon (fixed carbon) and mineral matter (ash), which can be distinguished by further heating the sample in the presence of oxygen. The carbon is converted to carbon dioxide leaving only the ash. Table 6.3 contains the proximate analysis (dry basis) of some biomass materials as well as fossil fuels for reference. It is noted that the relatively high volatile content of biomass, (50-75%) compared to coal (typically less than 25%) makes biomass very suitable for gasification. Gasification is a controlled process used to convert biomass into hydrogen and other gases without combustion. The relatively low ash content of biomass compared to coal also eases the ash disposal problems.

**Table 6.3:** Proximate analysis of some biomass

| Proximate analysis (%) | Coal | Sawdust | Groundnut | Rice Husk |
|---|---|---|---|---|
| Moisture | 5 | 10-20 | - | 10 |
| Volatile Matter | 25 | 50-70 | 73.3 | 55 |
| Fixed Carbon | 30 | 20-25 | 22.9 | 15 |
| Ash | 40 | 1-3 | 3.8 | 20 |

### 6.3.3 Ultimate Analysis

This processgives the elemental composition like carbon, hydrogen, oxygen, nitrogen, sulfur and chlorine along with moisture and ash contents in the biomass ongravimetric basis. Table 6.4presents the ultimate analysis of some biomass. From the table, it is seen that biomass on an average consists of 40-50% carbon, 4-7% hydrogen and 30-45% oxygen on moisture and ash free basis. Biomass also contains negligible amount of Nitrogen and Sulphur.

Heating value is the net energy released upon reaction of a particular fuel with oxygen under isothermal conditions (the starting and ending temperatures are the same). If the water vapors formed during reaction condense at the end of the process, the latent heat of condensation contributes to what is known as the higher heating value (HHV). If latent heat does not contribute, then the lower heating value (LHV) prevails. These measurements are typically performed in a bomb calorimeter and higher heating values of the biofuels are recorded. Heating values of biomass/biofuels are important in performing energy balances on biomass conversion process.

**Table 6.4:** Ultimate (elemental) analysis of some biomass

| Feedstock | C (%) | H (%) | N (%) | O (%) | Ash (%) |
|---|---|---|---|---|---|
| Wood | 44-52 | 5-7 | 0.5-0.9 | 40-48 | 1-3 |
| Rice Husk | 37 | 5.5 | 0.5 | 37 | 20 |
| Bagasse | 47 | 6.5 | 0.0 | 42.5 | 4 |
| Groundnut Shell | 34-45 | 2-4.6 | 1.1-1.4 | 43-60 | 3-5 |

**Properties of liquid fuel jatropha oil and biodiesel:**

Jatropha is a flowing plant and jatropha seeds are one of the widely used agro-seeds. Jatropha oil are mainly used for the production of biodiesel for the fuel requirements in remote rural area and forest communities. The properties of jatropha oil and biodiesel are given in Table 6.5.

**Table 6.5:** Properties of jatropha oil and biodiesel

| Properties | Jatropha oil | Jatropha biodiesel |
|---|---|---|
| Calorific value ($MJkg^{-1}$) | 38.65 | 39.23 |
| Density (15°C, $kgm^{-3}$) | 940 | 880 |
| Viscosity ($mm^2s^{-1}$) | 24.5 | 4.8 |
| Water content (%) | 1.4 | 0.025 |
| Ash content (%) | 0.8 | 0.012 |
| Carbon residue (%) | 1.0 | 0.20 |
| Acid value ($mgKOHg^{-1}$) | 28.0 | 0.40 |
| Flash point (°C) | 225 | 135 |
| Pour point (°C) | 4 | 2 |

**Properties of gaseous fuel biogas:**

Biogas is a gaseous fuel used for the production of electricity. It is an environmentally friendly renewable source of energy. Biogas is produced when organic matter like food and animal waste is broken down by microorganisms in the absence of oxygen. This process is called as anaerobic digestion. Biogas generally contains methane ($CH_4$), carbon dioxide ($CO_2$), hydrogen ($H_2$) and hydrogen sulphide ($H_2S$). The main properties of biogas and its components are presented in Table 6.6.

**Table 6.6:** Properties of biogas and its components

| Properties | Components | | | | Biogas (60% $CH_4$, 40% $CO_2$) |
|---|---|---|---|---|---|
| | $CH_4$ | $CO_2$ | $H_2$ | $H_2S$ | |
| Composition by volume (%) | 55-70 | 3.-45 | <1 | <3 | 100 |
| Calorific value (MJ.m$^{-3}$) | 37.7 | - | 10.8 | 22.8 | 22.6 |
| Density (kg.m$^{-3}$) | 0.72 | 1.98 | 0.09 | 1.54 | 1.2 |
| Flash point (°C) | 650-750 | - | 530-590 | 290-487 | 650-750 |
| Lower explosive limit (%) | 5-15 | - | 4-74 | 4-42 | 6-12 |
| Critical temperature (°C) | -82.5 | 31.0 | - | 100 | -82.5 |
| Critical pressure (MPa) | 4.6 | 7.3 | 1.3 | 8.9 | 7.3-8.9 |

## 6.4 BIOMASS BASED ELECTRIC POWER PLANTS

Based on the biomass conversion process used to generate electricity from the biomass, the biomass power plants can be classified as:

(i) Bio-chemical based (e.g. Biogas) powerplant
(ii) Thermo-chemical based (e.g. Municipal waste) power plant
(iii) Agro-chemical based (e.g. Bio-diesel) power plant

### 6.4.1 Bio-Chemical Based (e. g. Biogas) Power Plant:

In biochemical conversion, enzymes of bacteria and other micro-organisms are used to break the biomass. The layout of a biochemical based power plant is shown in Fig. 6.2.

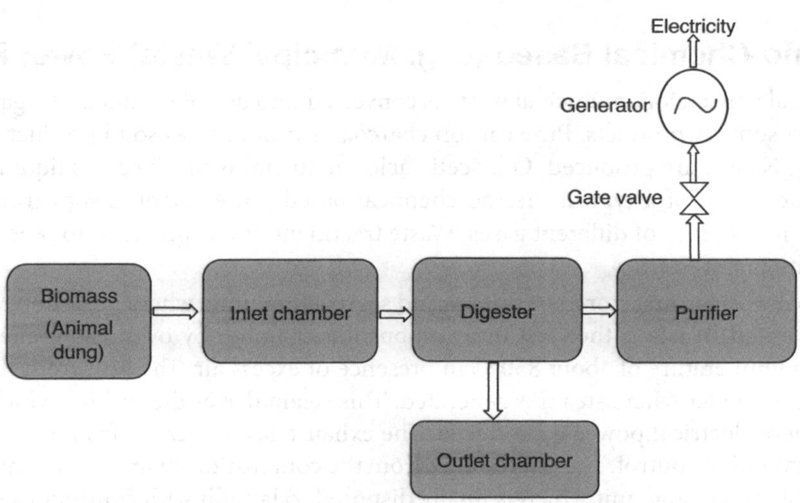


**Fig 6.2:** Layout of bio-chemical based (biogas) power plant

**Working of bio-chemical based power plant:**

Cattle dung is first mixed with water in the ratio of 1:1 in this inlet tank. This tank is connected to the digester with inlet pipe. Raw materials from the inlet tank are sent for anaerobic digestion in the digestion chamber. The waste coming from digester after fermentation are collected by in the outlet tank. In addition to the methane, biogas also contains some impurities like water vapour, carbon di-oxide and hydrogen sulfide.Hence a purifier is required to get pure biomethane. Biomethane flow from purifier to biogas generator where electricity is generated. Biogas generatorconsists of a combustion engine and a generator to transform energy into electrical power.

**Advantages of bio-chemical based power plant:**

1. It uses organic residues, waste materials, animal-dung which is available at very low cast in villages and small towns
2. Installation cost is low
3. The by-products are very useful
4. It is a renewable source of energy
5. It helps in employment generation and economic capacity building in small town and villages

The live picture of a biogas plant "Timokhovo",located about 40 km east of Moscow is shown in Fig. 6.3.

**Fig 6.3:** Biogas power plantlocated about 40 km east of Moscow
(**Photo:** Provided by electrosystems Co. Ltd.)

## 6.4.2 Thermo-Chemical Based (e. g. Municipal Waste) Power Plant

In thermo-chemical conversion, municipal waste is converted into useful products like gaseous & liquid fuels, residues and some byproducts. Pure carbon charcoal is produced as solid product. Gaseous fuels like $H_2$, CO, $CH_4$, $N_2$ etc. are produced. Oil, acetic acid, methanol is produced as liquid fuels in these power plants. The layout of a typical thermo-chemical based power plant is shown in Fig. 6.4. The biomass is heated in presence of different gases. Waste treatment unit is provided for energy conversion process from municipal waste.

The municipal waste is first stored in storage and segregation units where hazardous and recyclable materials are separated. Waste is then fed into combustion chamber by overhead cranes. It is burned there at very high temperature of about 850°C in presence of excess air. The heat from the combustion chamber is passed to boiler where steam is generated. This steam drives the turbine which is connected to a generator where electrical power is produced. The exhaust gases released from the boiler is sent to cleaning unit for pollution control. The ash residues from the combustion chamber and boiler are allowed to pass through ash processing unit which is finally disposed to landfill with continuous environmental monitoring.

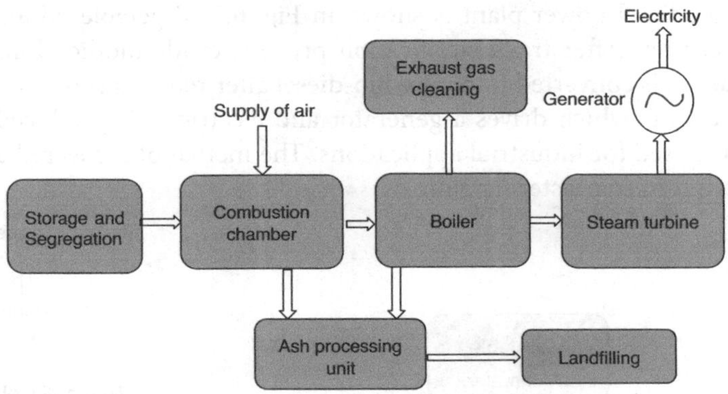


**Fig 6.4:** Layout of thermo-chemical based power plant

**Advantages of thermo-chemical based power plant:**

1. Heat produced can be used for various purposes
2. Landfill usage

The live picture of the South India's biggest plant at Jawahar Nagar dump yard to generate 20 MW of power through municipal solid waste in Hyderabad, India is shown in Fig. 6.5.

**Fig 6.5:** A20 MW municipal waste to energy plant at Jawahar Nagar, Hyderabad.

## 6.4.3 Agro-Chemical Based (e. g. Bio-Diesel) Power Plant

In agro-chemical based power plant, bio-diesel oil is produced by transesterification process of vegetable oil and animal fat. Jatropha, jojoba and karanja seeds are used as vegetable oils for production of biodiesel. The live picture of the biodiesel-based power plant in Belgium is shown in Fig. 6.6.

**Fig 6.6:** Waste-based biodiesel power plant in Belgium.

The layout of a biodiesel power plant is shown in Fig. 6.7. Vegetable oil and animal fats are fed into transesterification unit. After transesterification process, crude biodiesel and crude glycerin are obtained. Crude biodiesel is converted into pure bio-diesel after refining process. The bio-diesel is then used to run a diesel engine which drives a generator and electricity is produced. The crude glycerin after refining process is used for industrial applications. The methanol recovered after glycerin refining process is used as catalyst in transesterification.

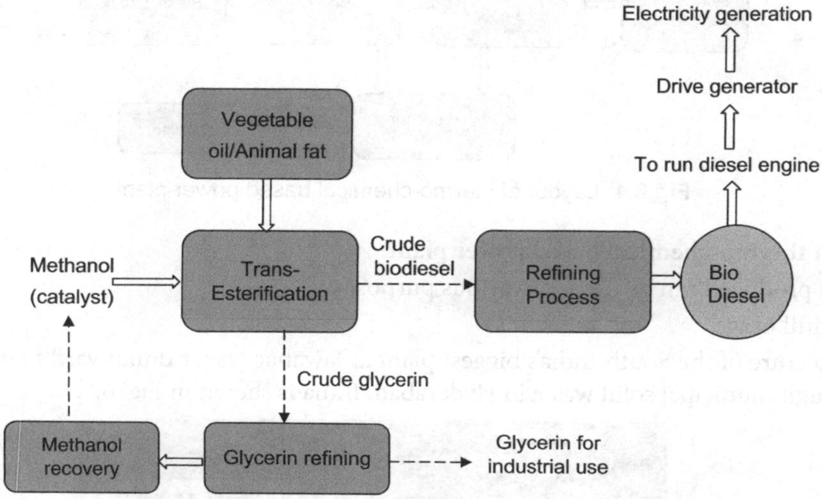


**Fig 6.7:** Layout of agro-chemical based power plant

**Advantages of agro-chemical based power plant:**

1. Clean and renewable alternative of petroleum diesel
2. Reduction is greenhouse gas emission

## UNIT SUMMARY

- Around 500 million tons of agriculture and agro-industrial residues is generated every year in India.
- Around 150 -200 million tons of biomass is available for electricity generation every year.
- Biomass is an organic matter comes from the living organisms like plants and animals.
- Biomass is produced as a result of the photosynthesis process.
- In photosynthesis the carbon dioxide ($CO_2$) and water ($H_2O$) combines together in presence of sun light and converted into an organic compound called biomass.
- The amount of biomass that can be obtained during the photosynthesis process depends on the availability of sunlight which drives the conversion of $CO_2$ and $H_2O$.
- Biomass used for the production of energy is called as biomass energy resources and the energy derived from biomass is called as biomass energy or biofuels.
- The main constituents of biomass energy resource are:

  (i) Lignin,

(ii) Hemicelluloses,
(iii) Cellulose,
(iv) Mineral matter and
(v) Ash.

- In biochemical conversion, enzymes of bacteria and other micro-organisms are used to break the biomass.
- In thermochemical conversion, municipal waste is converted into useful products like gaseous, liquid fuels, residues and some byproducts.
- In agro-chemical based power plant bio-diesel oil is produced by transesterification process of vegetable oil and animal fat.

# EXERCISES

## Multiple Choice Questions

1. Biomass is a
   (a) non-renewable source of energy
   (b) renewable source of energy
   (c) Both (a) and (b)
   (d) none of these
2. Biomass is produced as a result of
   (a) biosynthesis (b) photosynthesis
   (c) electrolysis (d) hydrolysis
3. Biomass is used in the production of
   (a) fibers (b) metals
   (c) bio-diesel (d) all of these
4. Whish agriculture residue can be utilized as a biomass
   (a) manure (b) fish oil
   (c) bagasse (d) none of these
5. Which of the following term is commonly used for biomass
   (a) inorganic matter (b) ammonium compound
   (c) chemicals (d) organic compound
6. Analysis to know thetypes and amounts of proteins, oils and sugarpresent in biomass
   (a) biochemical analysis (b) proximate analysis
   (c) ultimate analysis (d) gravimetric analysis
7. Biodiesel is produced in
   (a) thermo-chemical based power plant
   (b) agro-chemical based power plant
   (c) biochemical based power plant
   (d) electrochemical based power plant

**8.** Bio-diesel is produced as a result of

(a) photosynthesis (b) transesterification

(c) electrolysis (d) hydrolysis

**9.** Jatropha oil seeds are used to produce

(a) petrol (b) diesel

(c) biodiesel (d) natural gas

**10.** Which of the followings is not a biomass

(a) plants and trees (b) wood

(c) animal waste (d) water

| Answers of Multiple Choice Questions | | | | |
|---|---|---|---|---|
| 1. (b) | 2. (b) | 3. (c) | 4. (c) | 5. (d) |
| 6. (a) | 7. (b) | 8. (b) | 9. (c) | 10. (d) |

## Short and Long Answer Type Questions

### *Category I*

1. What is biomass and how it is useful?
2. Name various sources of biomass.
3. Define photosynthesis process.
4. Discuss biochemical and thermochemical conversion process.
5. How biodiesel is produced in agro-chemical based power plants.

### *Category II*

1. Discuss various types of biomass energy resources in details.
2. Discuss the properties of fuel used for electricity generation in biomass-based power plants.
3. Draw the layout of an agro-chemical based power plant. Discuss how the biodiesel is produced in these power plants.
4. With the help of a neat diagram explain the working of thermos-chemical based power plant.
5. Draw the layout of a biogas-based power plant and explain its working.

## PRACTICAL

## Assemble a small biogas plant to generate electric power.

**Aim:**

To assemble a small biogas plant to generate electric power.

**Theory:**

Schematic diagram a biogas-based power plant is shown in Fig. (i):

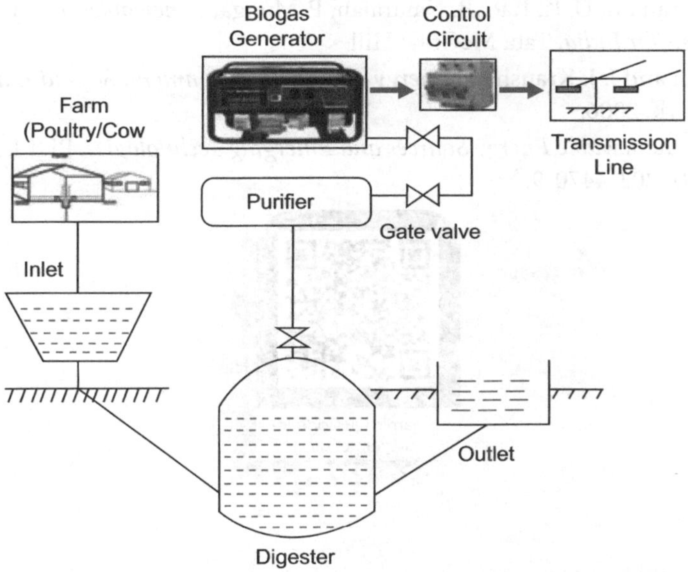


**Fig. (i):** Schematic diagram of a large head micro hydro power plant

**The components of abiogas-based power plant to be assembled are:**

(i) **Inlet tank:** Cattle dung is mixed with water in the ratio of 1:1 in this inlet tank. This tank is connected to the digester with inlet pipe.

(ii) **Digester:** It is an air-tight, waterproof container where raw materials from the inlet tank is sent for anaerobic digestion. It also includes a pipe to remove the digestate when fermentation is over.

(iii) **Outlet tank:** Outlet tank is required to collect all the waste coming from the digester.

(iv) **Purifier:** In addition to the methane biogas also contains some impurities like water vapour, carbon di-oxide and hydrogen sulfide. Hence a purifier is required to get pure biomethane.

(v) **Gate valve:** Gate valve allow biomethane to flow only in one direction from purifier to biogas generator.

(vi) **Biogas generator:** It consists of a combustion engine and a generator to transform energy into electrical power.

(vii) **Control circuit:** A control circuit is coupled between generator and transmission line. It controls the current flowing from generator to the transmission line.

**Conclusion:**

In this way one can assemble a small biogas plant to generate electric power.

## REFERENCES AND SUGGESTED READINGS

1. J. W. Twidella and A. Weir, *Renewable Energy Sources*, EFN Spon Ltd., UK, 2006.
2. Gipe, Paul: Wind Energy Basics, Chelsea Green Publishing Co; ISBN: 978- 1603580304
3. G. N. Tiwari and R. K. Mishra, *Advanced Renewable Energy Resources,* RSC Publishing, UK, 2012.

4. N. H. Ravindranath, U. K. Rao, B. Natarajan, P. Monga, *Renewable Energy and Environment-A Policy Analysis for India*, Tata McGraw Hill.
5. R. A. Ristinen and J. J. Kraushaar, *Energy and The Environment, Second Edition*, John Willey & Sons, New York, 2006.
6. D. P. Kothari, *Renewable Energy Sources and Emerging Technologies*, PHI Learning, New Delhi, ISBN: -978-81-203-4470-9.

Dynamic QR Code for Further Reading

# 7 Other Renewable Energy Sources

## UNIT SPECIFICS

In this unit, the power generation from tidal and wave energy is described. The ocean thermal energy conversion (OTEC) process is explained in detailed manner with the help of open and closed cycle systems. The process of hydro-geothermal conversion of electricity has been introduced. This unit also talk about hydrogen production processes and various methods of hydrogen storage has been. Fuel cell system and hybrid systems have been discussed in the unit. The advantages and disadvantages of OTEC system, geothermal is also listed in the unit.

Large answer type, short answer type and multiple-choice questions are given for better understanding of the readers. A list of references and suggested readings are given in the unit so that one can go through them for practice. It is important to note that for getting more information on various topics of interest some QR codes have been provided which can be scanned for relevant supportive knowledge.

## PRE-REQUISITES

Knowledge of various forms of energy (Class X)

## UNIT OUTCOMES

List of outcomes of this unit is as follows:

**U7-O1:** To learn about tidal and wave energy.

**U7-O2:** To understand open and closed cycle ocean thermal energy conversion (OTEC) system.

**U7-O3:** To study hydro-geothermal energy.

**U7-O4:** To study hydrogen energy and its storage.

**U7-O5:** To understand fuel cell systems.

| Unit-7 Outcomes | EXPECTED MAPPING WITH COURSE OUTCOMES (1-Weak Correlation;2-Medium Correlation; 3-Strong Correlation) | | | | |
|---|---|---|---|---|---|
| | CO-1 | CO-2 | CO-3 | CO-4 | CO-5 |
| U7-O1 | - | - | - | 2 | - |
| U7-O2 | - | - | - | 3 | - |
| U7-O3 | - | - | - | 2 | - |
| U7-O4 | - | - | - | - | - |
| U7-O5 | - | - | - | - | - |

## 7.1 TIDAL ENERGY

Gravitational interaction between Earth, the sun and the moon cause natural rise and fall in the sea water level. This regular change in the water level of sea and ocean is called tide. The rise and fall of water level is accompanied by periodic horizontal to and fro motion of water which is called as tidal currents. The tidal current flows in the horizontal direction and have kinetic energy. This energy is called as tidal current energy. The period between consecutive high tide is 12.5 hours.

This rise and fall are periodic in nature and follow a sinusoidal curve as shown in Fig. 7.1. The point A indicates high tide point and point B indicates low tide point.

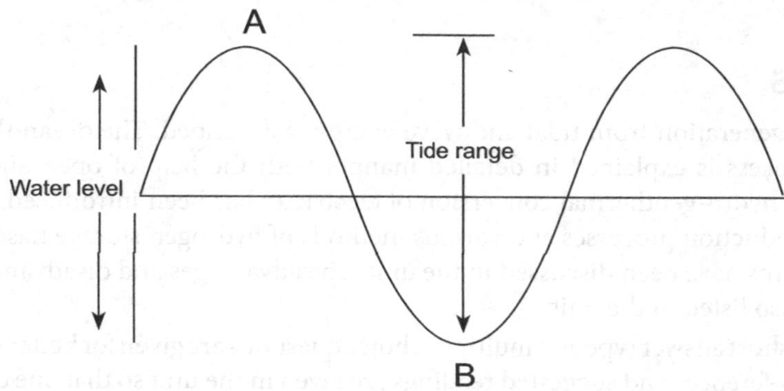


**Fig 7.1:** Rise and fall of the water level

The energy harnessed by converting the energy of tides into useful form of energy like electricity is called as tidal energy. Tidal energy is a form of renewable energy and has the great potential for future electricity generation.

There are very few locations in the world that are suitable for tidal energy generation. The list working tidal power stations in the world is shown in Table 7.1.

**Table 7.1:** Tidal power stations in operation

| Tidal power station | Generation capacity (MW) | Country |
|---|---|---|
| Sihwa Lake Tidal Power Station | 254 | South Korea |
| Rance Tidal Power Station | 240 | France |
| MeyGen Tidal Power Project | 6 | UK |
| Jiangxia Tidal Power Station | 3.2 | China |
| Kislaya Guba Tidal Power Station | 1.7 | Russia |
| Uldolmok Tidal Power Station | 1.5 | South Korea |
| Eastern Scheldt Barrier Tidal Power Station | 1.25 | Netherland |

Photograph of the world's largest Sihwa lake tidal power station, South Korea is shown in Fig. 7.2. This plant has the power generation capacity of about 254 MW. It consists of 10 eater turbine generators each with the installed generation capacity of 25.4 MW. The commercial operation of this plant began in 2011.

**Fig 7.2:** Sihwa Lake Tidal Power Station, South Korea (Courtesy: Shutterstock)

Tidal power projects of total capacity of 3 GW in England and up to 6 GW in Canada are under installation. India is also having great potential for tidal power generation. The possible location in India for tidal power exists in the Gulf of Kutch (Gujrat), Gulf of Combay (Bhavnagar) and in Sunderban area of West Bengal. The tidal power potential in India estimated to be around 9000 MW. The Central Electricity Authority of Gujrat has been planning to set up a 900 MW Kutch Tidal Power Project in Gujrat.

## 7.1.1 Tidal Power Plants

In tidal power plants, the water during high tide must be trapped behind a dam or barrage and then allowed to flee during the period of low tide. The water while fleeing is utilized to run a hydraulic turbine connected to a generator. The tide range of 5 m or above available in particular location can be used to run a hydraulic turbine. A tidal power plant must have the following main components:

(i) **Dam or Barrage:** The function of dam or barrage is to form a barrier between the sea and the basin or between one basin to another basin in case of multiple basins.

(ii) **Sluice gates:** These are the flow-controlled devices used to fill the basin during high tide and to empty the basin during low tide. In most of the tidal power plants, vertical lift gates are being used.

(iii) **Power house:** It contains equipment like turbine and generator.

Based on the basin used in plants, there are two types of tidal power plants

(1) Single Basin Tidal Power Plant

(2) Double Basin Tidal Power Plant

**(1) Single Basin Tidal Power Plants**

The single basin tidal power plants have only one basin. This is the simplest system to generate tidal power. The basin and sea are separated by a dam. The rise and fall of the water level provides the potential head. The sluice gate is opened during the high tide to fill the basin. The general arrangement of a double cycle single basin tidal power plant is shown in Fig. 7.3. These plants generally use reversible water turbines in order to generate power during filling and emptying of the basin. Filling of the basin occurs when the sea is at high tide level and water in the basin is at low tide level. The emptying of basin occurs when basin is at high tide level and sea is at low tide. The flow of water in both the directions is used to run the water turbine.

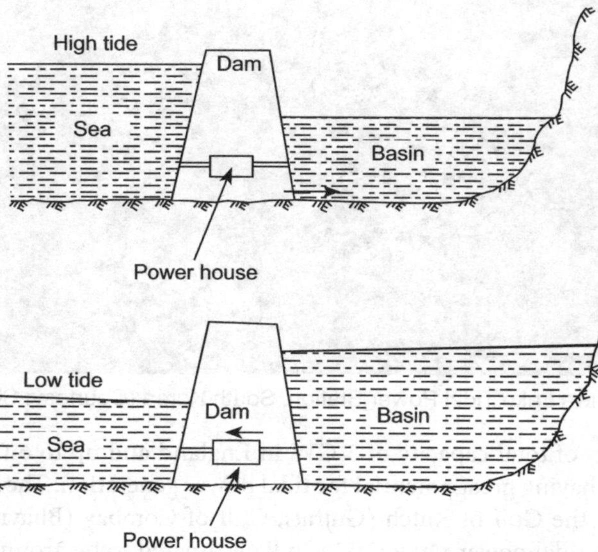


Fig 7.3: Single basin power plant during high and low tide

**(2) Double Basin Tidal Power Plants**

The general arrangement of a double basin tidal power plant is shown in Fig. 7.4. In double basin plant, there are two basins at different levels. Basin situated in the upper part is called as upper basin and other situated in the lower portion is called as lower basin. A dam is constructed between the two basins. The dam also contains the power house. Two sluice gates are provided in the dam. Gate connecting the sea to the upper basin is known as inlet sluice gate and that connecting the sea to the lower basin is called as outlet sluice gate. The upper basin is filled with water during flood tide. When tide reaches its peak value, the inlet sluice gate is then closed. Water flows from upper basin to the lower basin through the turbines and then the turbine starts running and power is generated. The water flow is controlled in such a way that continuous power is obtained from the plant. As water flows from upper basin to lower basin, the water level in upper basin falls and that in lower basin rises. When the rising level in lower basin becomes equal to the level of falling tide, the outlet sluice gates are opened.

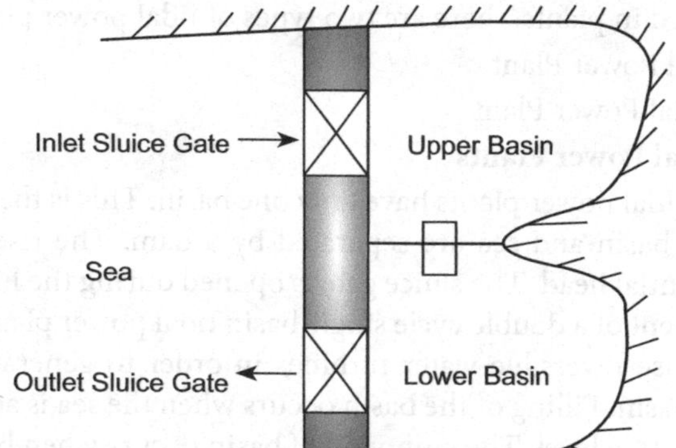


Fig 7.4: Double basin power plant

### 7.1.2 Advantages and Disadvantages of Tidal Power Plant

**Advantages:**

(i) It is free from pollution as it does not use any fuel.

(ii) No extra valuable land is required.

(iii) It does not produce any unhealthy gas or ash.

(iv) It is everlasting and is not influenced by the changing mood of the nature like failure of monsoon.

**Disadvantages:**

(i) Power generation is not uniform due to variation in tidal range.

(ii) It is difficult to do construction in sea.

(iii) There is a chance of corrosion of the machinery due to corrosive sea water.

(iv) The cost of power transmission is high because the tidal power plants are located away from the load centers.

## 7.2 WAVE ENERGY

Ocean waves contains huge amount of energy and power. Ocean waves are generated as a result of blowing of winds over the surface of sea. The energy (or power) captured from the ocean waves is called as wave energy (or wave power). The wave power is produced by the up and down motion of the floating devices placed on the surface of ocean. In certain parts of the world, availability of this wave energy is very vast and the development of devices for harnessing the wave power from ocean is quite important. There are two main types of wave energy generators.

(1) **Fixed devices:** The arrangement of a fixed type wave energy generator is shown in Fig. 7.5. The wave reaching the sea shore is being used like a piston to push air up and down a large pipe. Strong concrete wall is constructed half in and half out of the water. This wall traps a column of air inside the machine. As the wave rushes in, the air is forced to move in the upward direction and spins the turbine. As the wave retreats, air is sucked back through the turbine, causing it to spin once again. The turbine is connected to a generator, which produces electricity.

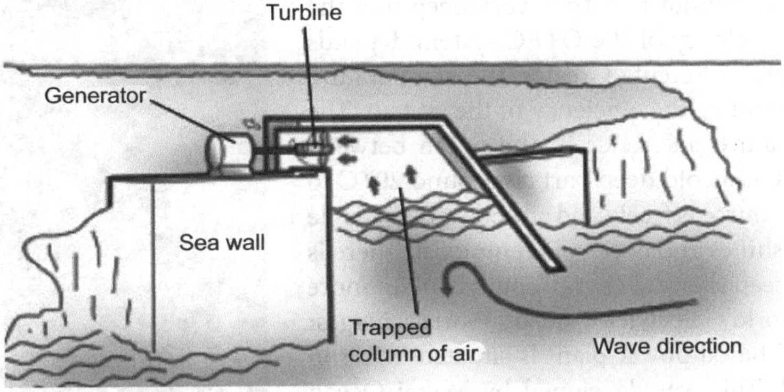


**Fig 7.5:** Arrangement of a fixed type energy generator

(2) **Floating devices:** These are generally found offshore. It consists of a series of large size metal tubes joined together with flexible hinges. The movement of the waves causes section of these

tubes to move up and down. Each hinge is connected to a pump which pumps oil through a hydraulic motor as it moves. The motor generates electricity as it spins. The arrangement of a typical floating device is shown in Fig. 7.6.

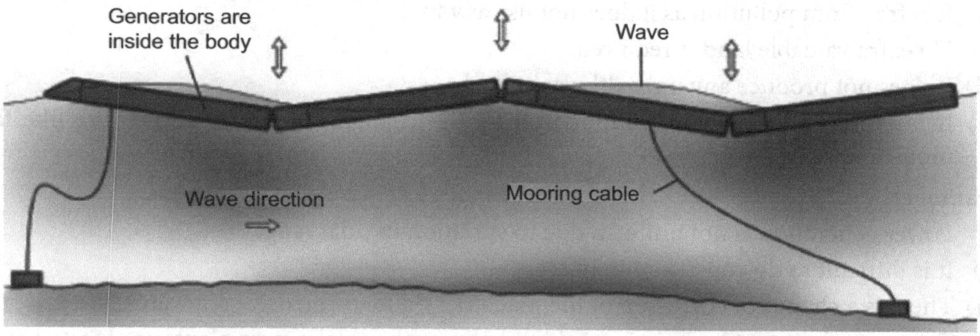


**Fig 7.6:** Arrangement of a floating type energy generator

## 7.2.1 Potential of Wave Power Generation

The worldwide potential of wave energy is estimated to be more than 2 TW (Terawatt). The potential locations for wave power generation includes the western seaboard of Europe, the northern coast of UK, the pacific coastlines of North and South America, South Africa, Australia and New Zealand. As per an estimate given by National Renewable Energy Laboratory (NREL), the annual wave energy potential of US is 1170 TWh (Terawatt hour). According to a report shared by ministry of New and Renewable Energy (MNRE), India the estimated theoretical wave power potential in India in about 41300 MW.

## 7.3 OCEAN THERMAL ENERGY CONVERSION (OTEC)

Ocean thermal energy conversion (OTEC) system uses the temperature difference between the warm shallow part of the ocean water and cold deep ocean water to generate electricity. The deeper parts of the ocean are cooler because the sunlight cannot penetrate very deep into the ocean water. The efficiency of the OTEC system depends on the temperature different. Greater the temperature difference, greater will be the efficiency of the system. The maximum temperature difference in the ocean between warm shallow part and cold deep parts is around 20° C to 25° C. This energy source is freely and abundantly available as long as the sun shines and ocean currents exist. There is an estimate that ocean thermal energy could contain more than twice the world's electricity need. World's biggest operational OTEC based power plant is situated in US in shown in Fig. 7.7. This was developed by Makai Ocean Engineering. The annual power generation capacity of this plant is 100 kW and this is sufficient to power 120 homes in Hawaii, US.

**Fig 7.7:** World's biggest operational OTEC based power plant is situated in US
(**Source:** Wikimedia Commons)

### 7.3.1 Types of OTEC System

There are two types of OTEC power generation system. One is open cycle or Claude cycle OTEC system and other is closed cycle or Anderson cycle OTEC system. The OTEC power generation plant generally consists of a working fluid, evaporator, turbine, condenser and pump.

**(1) Open Cycle or Claude Cycle OTEC system**

In this system, sea water works as the working fluid. Warm ocean water from the shallow part is pumped into a flash evaporator. The pressure is lowered by a vacuum pump to the point where the warm sea water boils at ambient temperature. This process produces steam. This steam is used to run a low-pressure turbo-generator which generates electricity. After leaving the turbine, the steam is condensed in a heat exchanger with the help of cold deep ocean water. It also produces desalinated water. Arrangement of an open-cycle OTEC process is shown in Fig.7.8.

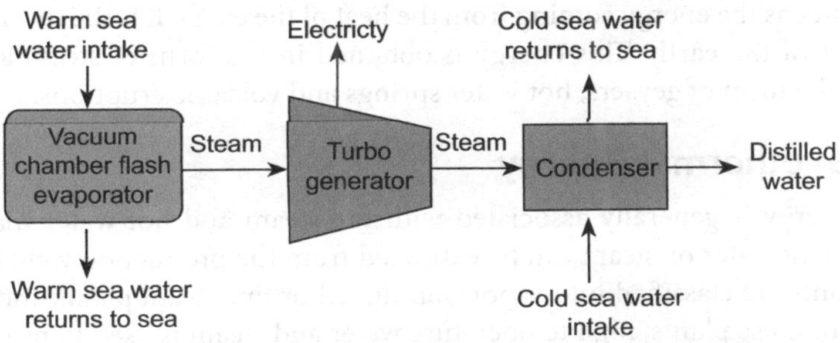


**Fig 7.8:** Arrangement of open cycle OTEC system

**(2) Closed Cycle or Anderson cycle OTEC system**

In closed cycle system low boiling liquid like ammonia or Freon is used as working fluid. The fluid is heated and then vaporized in a heat exchanger with the help of warm surface sea water. The steam produced drives a steam turbine generator. After passing through the steam turbine, the exhausted steam is condensed in another heat exchanger. It is cooled by water drawn from the deep ocean. The working fluid is then pumped back through the warm water heat exchanger. The cycle is repeated continuously. The arrangement of a closed-cycle OTEC system is shown in Fig. 7.9.

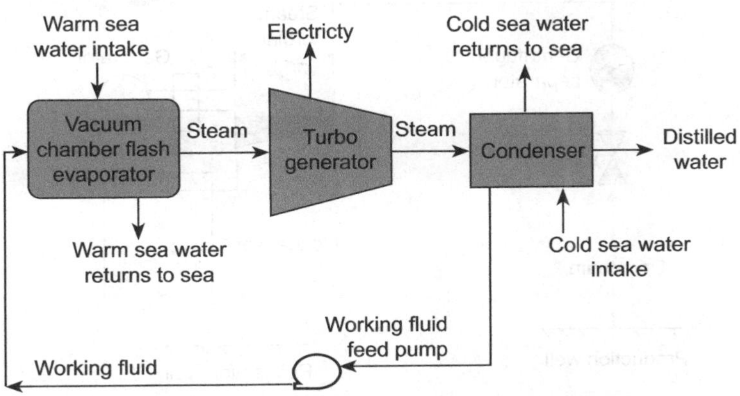


**Fig 7.9:** Arrangement of closed cycle OTEC system

### 7.3.2 Advantages and Disadvantages of OTEC Systems

**Advantages:**

(i) OTEC is a kind of renewable energy source

(ii) It can be used continuously for 24 hours throughout the year.

(iii) Produces electricity without emission of greenhouse gases.

**Disadvantages:**

(i) The installation and running costs are high.

(ii) Causes disturbances in aquatic and marine life.

(iii) Low conversion efficiency of about 3- 5%.

## 7.4 GEOTHERMAL ENERGY

Geothermal energy means the energy coming from the heat of the earth. It is the thermal energy trapped within the solid crust of the earth. This energy is obtained in the form of steam and hot water. It is released naturally in the form of geysers, hot water springs and volcanic eruptions.

### 7.4.1 Hydro-Geothermal Energy

Hydro-geothermal energy is generally associated with the steam and hot water that comes from the interior of the earth. Hot water or steam can be extracted from the production well. Hydro-geothermal power generation plants are classified into vapor dominated or dry steam plants and liquid dominated or wet steam plants. In these plants, high temperature water and steam is used to produce electricity.

(i) **Vapour Dominated or Dry Steam Plants:**

These plants are simple and more efficient type of hydro-geothermal power plants. The geothermal fluid for these plants is dry steam at temperatures between 180° C to 240° C. The schematic diagram of a vapour dominated power plant is shown in Fig. 7.10. Dry steam from the production well is passed to a centrifugal separator through valve. The centrifugal separator removes the impurities present in the steam. The steam is then allowed to pass through a steam turbine where steam expands and run the turbine. Turbine is connected to a generator where electricity is produced. The low pressure steam is condensed in to water and reinjected into the earth trough reinjection well.

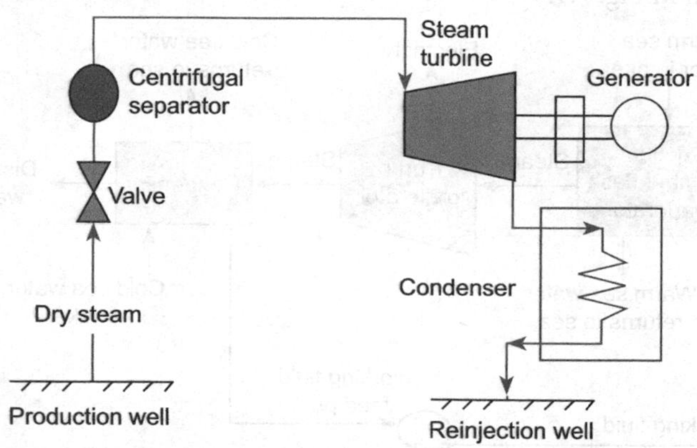


**Fig 7.10:** Schematic diagram of vapour dominated plant

**(ii) Liquid Dominated or Flash Steam Plants:**

In these plants, the mixture of hot water and steam under high pressure is used. The steam is separated and expands in the turbine to generate electricity. There are two types of wet steam power plants.

(a) Single flash steam plant

(b) Double flash steam plant

(a) **Single flash steam plant:**

The schematic diagram of a single flash steam plant is shown in Fig. 7.11. In this plant, mixture of steam and hot water extracted from the production well is passed through flash separator by decreasing its pressure. In flash separator steam is separated from hot water and transmitted to the steam turbine to run it. Turbine is connected to a mechanical generator where electricity is produced. The cooled steam in the turbine is condensed into water by the condenser. A part of liquid from the flash separator is reinjected to the injection well.

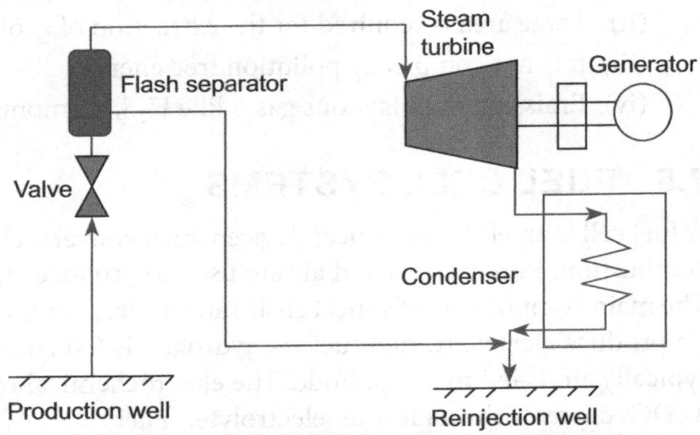


**Fig 7.11:** Schematic diagram of a single flash plant

(b) **Double flash steam plant:**

In double flash steam plant, the flash process of fluid is applied in two separators. Schematic diagram of the double flash power plant is shown in Fig. 7.12. The fluid flows from production well to a high-pressure flash separator through a valve where steam is separated and is piped to a two-stage turbine. Turbine is connected to a generator where electricity is produced. The exhausted steam in the turbine is condensed into water by the condenser. A part of liquid from the flash separator is reinjected to the injection well.

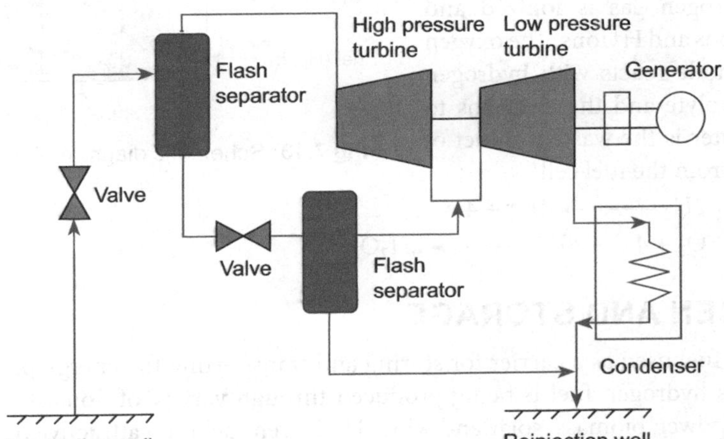


**Fig 7.12:** Schematic diagram of a double flash plant

### 7.4.2 Advantages and Disadvantages of Geothermal Power Generation

**Advantages:**

(i) Inexhaustive and available throughout the year.

(ii) Cheaper as compared with energies obtained from other sources.

(iii) Does not involve combustion of any fossil fuel.

(iv) Hot water can directly be used for space heating.

**Disadvantages:**

(i) It causes thermal pollution.

(ii) Large area is required for the extraction of geothermal energy.

(iii) It is not completely pollution free energy.

(iv) Emission of poisonous gases like $H_2S$, ammonia, methene and $CO_2$.

## 7.5 FUEL CELL SYSTEMS

A fuel cell is an electrochemical device which converts chemical energy into electricity and heat without combustion. Pure oxygen and air are used to produce electricity with water and oxygen as bi-products. The main components of a fuel cell are an anode, a cathode and an electrolyte sandwiched between them. To produce electricity, fuel such as hydrogen is fed continuously to the anode, and an oxidizing agent, typically air, is fed to the cathode. The electrochemical reactions take place at the electrodes, producing a DC current through the electrolyte. Fuel cell works like a battery. But unlike a battery, which consumes its reactants and oxidant and must be recharged when depleted, a fuel cell will continue to produce electricity as long as fuel and oxygen are supplied to the cell. The schematic diagram of a fuel cell is shown in Fig. 7.13.

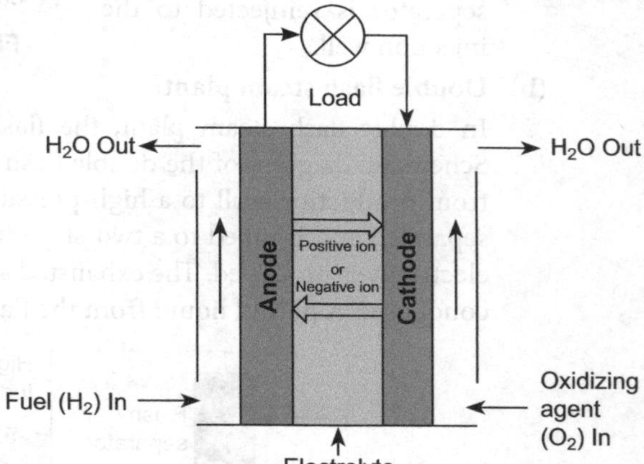


**Fig 7.13:** Schematic diagram of a hydrogen fuel cell

The operation of a fuel cell is as follows:

At anode, hydrogen gas is ionized and produces free electrons and $H^+$ ions. The oxygen supplied to the cathode reacts with hydrogen ions from the electrolyte and the electrons to give water. Thus, water is the waste product of the cell flowing out from the fuel cell.

At Anode: $2H_2 \longrightarrow 4H^+ + 4e^-$

At Cathode: $O_2 + 4e^- + 4H^+ \longrightarrow 2H_2O$

## 7.6 HYDROGEN AND STORAGE

Hydrogen is a clean fuel used as a carrier for storing and transporting the energy produced from other sources. Now a days hydrogen fuel is being produced through variety of domestic resources such as natural gas, nuclear power, biomass, solar and wind. Hydrogen fuel is an attractive option for electricity generation and transportation applications. It can also be used in cars, in houses and in many other applications.

### 7.6.1 Hydrogen Production

Today, hydrogen fuel can be produced through several processes like thermochemical process, electrolytic process, solar water splitting process and biological process.

**(i) Thermochemical Processes:**

Thermochemical process uses heat and chemical reactions to release hydrogen from organic materials like biomass or from materials like water. Natural gas reforming is a thermochemical process used for the production of hydrogen. In this process, the methane ($CH_4$) contained in natural gas is used to produce hydrogen with thermal process such as steam-methane reformation and partial oxidation. In steam-methane reformation, methane reacts with steam in the presence of a catalyst to produce hydrogen ($H_2$), carbon monoxide (CO), carbon-oxide ($CO_2$). Further, the carbon mono-oxide reacts with steam in the presence of a catalyst to produce carbon di-oxide and more hydrogen. This reaction is called as water-gas shift reaction.

**Steam-methane reforming reaction:**

$$CH_4 + H_2O + \text{heat} \rightarrow CO + 3H_2$$

**Water-gas shift reaction:**

$$CO + H_2O \rightarrow CO_2 + H_2 + \text{small amount of heat}$$

**(ii) Electrolytic Process:**

Water can also be separated into hydrogen ($H_2$) and Oxygen ($O_2$)using electrolysis. Electrolyzer uses electricity to split water into hydrogen and oxygen. This technology is well developed and is available commercially. In this process, water reacts at anode to form oxygen and hydrogen ions ($H^+$). The electrons flow through the external circuit and the hydrogen ions moves across the electrolyte from anode to the cathode. At cathode, hydrogen ions combine with the electrons from the external circuit to form hydrogen molecule ($H_2$).

**At anode:** $2H_2O \rightarrow O_2 + 4H^+ + 4e^-$

**At cathode:** $4H^+ + 4e^- \rightarrow 2H_2$

**(iii) Solar Water Splitting Process:**

This process is also called as photolytic process. In this process light energy is used to split water into hydrogen and oxygen. This process is currently under early stage of research and not a commercial way to produce hydrogen.

**(iv) Biological Process:**

In this process, microbes like bacteria and microalgae are used to produce hydrogen through biological reaction using sunlight and organic matter. This technology is still in research and development stage. But expected to have a great potential for sustainable hydrogen production.

### 7.6.2 Hydrogen Storage

Hydrogen storage is very important for advancement of hydrogen and fuel cell technology. Hydrogen has the highest energy per unit mass but because of its low ambient temperature density, the energy per unit volume is low. Therefore, it requires advanced storage methods that have the potential for higher energy density. Hydrogen can be stored physically in the form of gas or a liquid. Hydrogen storage as gas requires high-pressure tanks of about pressure of 350-700 bar. Since boiling temperature of hydrogen at one atmospheric pressure of about -252.8°C, the hydrogen storage as liquid requires cryogenic temperature. Hydrogen can also be stored on the surface of solids by adsorption or within the solids by absorption (known as hydrates). Hydrogen storage in solids involves the use of metal hydrides and some carbon-based materials.

Major challenges with hydrogen storage are that it is not easy to store hydrogen because of its low volume energy density. It can easily be lost in the atmosphere because if its lighter weight. Hydrogen is the lightest of all the elements.

## 7.7 HYBRID SYSTEMS

In hybrid systems two or more energy conversion devices combined together for power generation. These are specially preferred in remote areas for producing electrical power. A typical hybrid system is consisted of photovoltaics, small wind generators, fuel cell and a battery bank installed together for provide electricity in selected areas. The block diagram of a hybrid system is illustrated in Fig. 7.14. The system consists of a PV array which converts solar energy into electrical energy (DC power), wind turbine which converts kinetic energy of wind into mechanical energy and with the help of a DC generator this mechanical energy is converted into DC power. The main controller ensures the continues power supply to the home load. A fuel cell generator and battery banks are used to supply energy when needed and to store it when not needed.

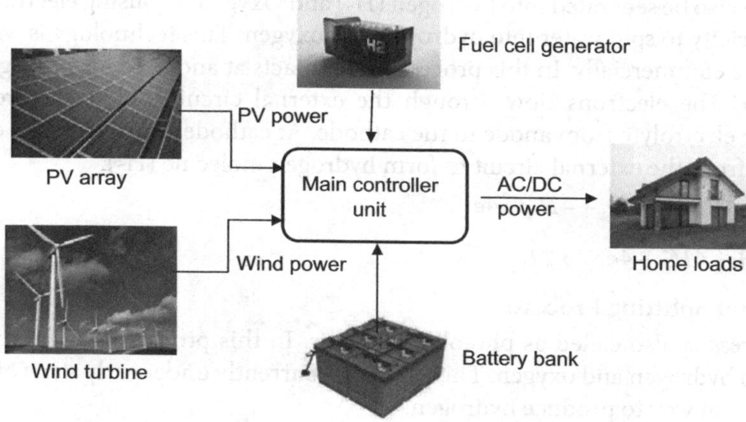


**Fig 7.14:** Block diagram of a hybrid power generation system

### 7.7.1 Advantages and Disadvantages of Hybrid Systems

**Advantages:**

(i) Low fossil fuel consumption due to use of renewable energy sources.

(ii) Most economical in case of higher fuel price

(iii) Low environmental impact because of the use of renewable energy sources

**Disadvantages:**

(i) Installation cost is high because of the use of renewable energy sources

(ii) Maintenance cost if high because of the presence of large number of different components.

(iii) Hybrid systems are still in research and development stage and is new of the users

## UNIT SUMMARY

- The energy harnessed by converting the energy of tides into useful form of energy like electricity is called as tidal energy.
- Ocean waves contains huge amount of energy and power. Ocean waves are generated as a result of blowing of winds over the surface of sea.
- The energy (or power) captured from the ocean waves is called as wave energy (or wave power).
- Ocean thermal energy conversion (OTEC) system uses the temperature difference between the warm shallow part of the ocean water and cold deep ocean water to generate electricity.
- The maximum temperature difference in the ocean between warm shallow part and cold deep parts is around 20°C to 25°C.
- In open cycle OTEC system, sea water works as the working fluid.
- In closed cycle OTEC system, low boiling liquid like ammonia or Freon is used as working fluid.
- Geothermal energy is the energy coming from the heat of the earth. It is the thermal energy trapped within the solid crust of the earth.
- Hydro-geothermal energy is generally associated with the steam and hot water that comes from the interior of the earth.
- Dry steam plants are simple and more efficient type of hydro-geothermal power plants. The geothermal fluid for these plants is dry steam at temperatures between 180°C to 240°C.
- In flash steam plants, the mixture of hot water and steam under high pressure is used. The steam is separated and expands in the turbine to generate electricity.
- A fuel cell is an electrochemical device which converts chemical energy into electricity and heat without combustion.
- Hydrogen is a clean fuel used as a carrier for storing and transporting the energy produced from other sources.
- Hydrogen storage is very important for advancement of hydrogen and fuel cell technology. Hydrogen has the highest energy per unit mass.
- Hydrogen storage as gas requires high-pressure tanks of about pressure of 350-700 bar.
- Since boiling temperature of hydrogen at one atmospheric pressure of about -252.8°C, the hydrogen storage as liquid requires cryogenic temperature.
- In hybrid systems two or more energy conversion devices combined together for power generation.

## EXERCISES

### Multiple Choice Questions

1. The tide range required to run a hydraulic turbine is.
   (a) 2 meter or below  (b) 5 meter or above
   (c) 10 meter or above  (d) All of these

2. Energy derived from the hot spots beneath the earth is called
   (a) bioenergy (b) ocean energy
   (c) geothermal energy (d) solar energy
3. Geothermal energy is extracted from
   (a) sun (b) earth
   (c) sea (d) sky
4. The maximum temperature difference in the ocean between warm shallow part and cold deep parts is around
   (a) less than 20°C (b) greater than 25°C
   (c) 20°C to 25°C (d) greater than 100°C
5. The solar intensity with water depth
   (a) increases (b) decreases
   (c) remain constant (d) none of these
6. The energy captured from the ocean waves is called as
   (a) wave energy (b) nuclear energy
   (c) solar energy (d) geothermal energy
7. What type of energy is a wave energy
   (a) renewable energy (b) non-renewable energy
   (c) commercial (d) none of these
8. Chemical energy is converted into..................... energy by a fuel cell
   (a) solar (b) potential
   (c) electrical (d) mechanical
9. Which of the following use hydrogen as fuel?
   (a) fossil fuels (b) fuel cells
   (c) photosynthesis (d) cooking
10. What is a fuel cell
   (a) converts heat energy to chemical energy
   (b) converts heat energy to electrical energy
   (c) converts chemical energy to electrical energy
   (d) converts kinetic energy to heat energy

| Answers of Multiple Choice Questions | | | | |
|---|---|---|---|---|
| 1. (b) | 2. (c) | 3. (b) | 4. (c) | 5. (b) |
| 6. (a) | 7. (a) | 8. (c) | 9. (b) | 10. (c) |

## Short and Long Answer Type Questions

### *Category I*

1. What do you mean by dry steam and wet steam?
2. What are different sources of geothermal energy?

3. Define tidal energy and wave energy.
4. What is fuel cell?
5. Define the hybrid system.

### *Category II*

1. Describe the working of open cycle OTEC power plant.
2. Describe single flash liquid dominated geothermal power plant.
3. Explain the working of double basin tidal system with the help of neat diagram.
4. Discuss various methods of hydrogen production.
5. Discuss the working of fuel cell with the help of a neat diagram.

## REFERENCES AND SUGGESTED READINGS


1. Twidell, J.W. & Weir, A., Renewable Energy Sources, EFN Spon Ltd., UK, 2006.
2. Sukhatme. S.P., Solar Energy, Tata McGraw Hill Publishing Company Ltd., New Delhi, 1997.
3. Godfrey Boyle, Renewable Energy, Power for a Sustainable Future, Oxford University Press, U.K., 1996.
4. NH Ravindranath, UK Rao, B Natarajan, P Monga,Renewable Energy and Environment-A Policy Analysis for India, Tata McGraw Hill.
5. RA Ristinen and J J Kraushaar,Energy and The Environment, Second Edition, John Willey & Sons, New York, 2006.
6. G. N. Tiwari and R. K. Mishra, *Advanced Renewable Energy Resources,* RSC Publishing, UK, 2012.
7. D. P. Kothari, *Renewable Energy Sources and Emerging Technologies*, PHI Learning, New Delhi, ISBN: -978-81-203-4470-9.
8. GN Tiwari and MK Ghoshal, Fundamental of Renewable Energy Sources, Narosa, New Delhi, 2007.


Dynamic QR Code for Further Reading

## CO AND PO ATTAINMENT TABLE

Course outcomes (COs) for this course can be mapped with the programme outcomes (POs) after the completion of the course and a correlation can be made for the attainment of POs to analyze the gap. After proper analysis of the gap in the attainment of POs necessary measures can be taken to overcome the gaps.

**Table for CO and PO attainment**

| Course Outcomes | ATTAINMENT OF PROGRAMME OUTCOMES (1- Weak Correlation; 2- Medium Correlation; 3- Strong Correlation) | | | | | | |
|---|---|---|---|---|---|---|---|
| | PO-1 | PO-2 | PO-3 | PO-4 | PO-5 | PO-6 | PO-7 |
| CO-1 | | | | | | | |
| CO-2 | | | | | | | |
| CO-3 | | | | | | | |
| CO-4 | | | | | | | |
| CO-5 | | | | | | | |

The data filled in the above table can be used for gap analysis.